7452 KLA

7452 KLA

PLAY ALL DAY Design for Children

gestalten

TABLE OF CONTENTS

PREFACE

What do children need to grow up in the best possible way?

How do they become self-confident, healthy personalities?

What leads to a child having a sheltered childhood?

When it comes to children and their education, one should keep things as simple as possible. Without favouring any of today's many popular educational theories and ideological directions pretending to know it all, there are three widely undisputed things that are important for a child's healthy development: Challenging tasks to grow from, good examples to learn from and a nurturing community/environment that makes them feel at home.

> The world in which children grow up today is very different from the childhood that most of the 30+ adults experienced when they were kids. Media and technology have made quantum leaps that keep constantly changing our perception as much as they alter our ways of dealing with the objective world. The traditional family split up. Single mothers and single dads take turns with family responsibilities, sometimes developing into patchwork families, while job-wise only a very few keep the same profession for their entire life. People also move house far more frequently than they used to, which means that children have to face difficult topics in regard to tolerance and flexibility, since they leave and lose their circle of friends and have to settle in new environments. Consequently, 'learning for life' means being able to comprehend complex networks rather than linear structures. Self confidence, flexibility and a proactive approach are essential.

The framework within which these attributes can evolve and thrive must be defined and redefined at regular (and irregular) intervals. Amidst those loosely connected relations and uncertain structures, the most reliable and valuable gift parents can give to their children is time. PLAY ALL DAY addresses new ways of designing the phenotypes of such frameworks in the chapters Playgrounds and Home Sweet Home. While Exploration and Express Yourself farm the fertile grounds of children's (leisure) time and (self-)expression, the introductory chapter Let's Play presents toys, puppets and characters from the intersection of the aforementioned, highlighting recent trends towards homemade objects that are perfect examples of parents joining forces with kids to enhance creativity and autonomy.

> PLAY ALL DAY is a book for children, parents and everyone who works with and for kids. While playing and improvising are being increasingly discussed and highlighted at design conferences the world over as methodical premises for the solution of all kinds of problems, it becomes clear that the children's room will always remain a hotbed for new ideas and creative experimentation. Why that? Because children see toys in a myriad of things. And, of course, because children take play seriously.

Life's a game – let's play all day…

LET'S PLAY

The recent revival of DIY culture has led to the design of exciting hand or self-made toys as well as hilarious new interpretations of toy classics that are full of strong expression and self-awareness.

Along with the rediscovery of modular systems that make toys more flexible and playable in a variety of ways, new small labels are coming up with fresh ideas and new ways to design dolls and toys. These designers and artists do not necessarily care about the symmetry of limbs, harmony of proportions or the functionality of their creations. Far from it! These imperfect toys present their own history rather than following someone else's story. Just look at the provocative yet funny injured dolls of Joshua Ben Longo, take herzensart's almost pathetic Vikings and knights who seem to be more frightened than terrifying or the sassy, bold figures of character pioneers FriendsWithYou - as much as they are less «pretty» than their flawless ancestors, they definitely stand for originality and personality.

These cute and insecure looking role-models are arriving on tiptoe to introduce ideas of tolerance and respect; trying out the not-so-obvious by subtly playing with forms. This means that while classics like Lego might still be eligible, new tactile toys are appealing to children as a superior means of learning and developing, encouraging them to use their hands and imagination, to cultivate skills and craftsmanship and to experiment with (recycled) materials. More often than not, they are joined by parents who have realised that time is the most valuable gift they can give to their children.

As Arounna Khounnoraj, who makes textiles and artwork that explore sculpture, drawing and printmaking, pattern and image, along with kids' objects, points out: 'My projects tend to be process-based rather than skill-based. They take advantage of anybody's ability to make marks, but still leave room for personal gestures and directions. There is a link between the two, a similar sensibility; my philosophy is that there shouldn't be much of a distinction between things for children and things for adults.' Insofar, playing does not only challenge the abilities of children (and grown-ups alike!), it also shapes the senses.

1

1. — **Marilyn Neuhart** 2007, *Mary Evelyn* ^{Design} / <u>Marilyn Neuhart</u> ^{Photographer} / <u>Andrew Neuhart</u> ^{Material} / Mexican cotton ^{Description} / 9-inch stuffed doll.

2. — 2006, *Mermaid Meryl* ^{Design} / <u>Marilyn Neuhart</u> ^{Photographer} / <u>Andrew Neuhart</u> ^{Material} / Mexican cotton ^{Description} / 14-inch stuffed doll.

3. — 2007, *Marian Eleanor* ^{Design} / <u>Marilyn Neuhart</u> ^{Photographer} / <u>Andrew Neuhart</u> ^{Material} / Mexican cotton ^{Description} / 10-inch stuffed doll.

4. — 2004, *Jones Lion* ^{Design} / <u>Marilyn Neuhart</u> ^{Photographer} / <u>Andrew Neuhart</u> ^{Material} / Mexican cotton ^{Description} / 11-inch stuffed doll.

- 2 -

- 3 -

- 4 -

- 1 -

1. — **blabla Kids** 2007, *Boogaloos* ^{Design} / <u>Florence Wetterwald</u>
^{Manufacturer} / <u>blabla</u> ^{Material} / Hand knit 100% cotton.

2. — 2007, *Charles* ^{Design} / <u>Florence Wetterwald</u> ^{Manufacturer} / blabla
^{Material} / Hand knit 100% cotton ^{Description} / Giant doll.

3. — 2007, *Finger Puppets* ^{Design} / <u>Florence Wetterwald</u>
^{Manufacturer} / <u>blabla</u> ^{Material} / 100% cotton.

- 2 -

- 3 -

- 4 -

- 5 -

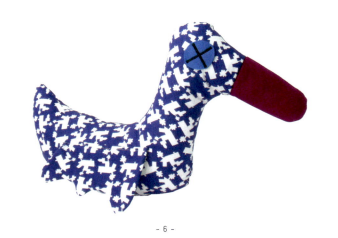

- 6 -

4. — **Tas-ka** 2008, *Monster* ^Design^ / <u>Hester Worst, Jantien Baas</u> ^Material^ / Cotton, Wool felt.

5. — 2008, *Monster pink* ^Design^ / <u>Hester Worst, Jantien Baas</u> ^Photography^ / <u>Hester Worst, Jantien Baas</u> ^Material^ / Cotton, Wool felt.

6. — 2008, *Duck Blue* ^Design^ / <u>Hester Worst, Jantien Baas</u> ^Photography^ / <u>Hester Worst, Jantien Baas</u> ^Material^ / Cotton, Wool felt.

7. **Judith Drews** — 2007, *Sockmonkey Pierre* ^Design^ / <u>Judith Drews</u> ^Material^ / Socks.

8. — **Lizette Greco** 2006, *Hello Man* ^Design^ / <u>Lizette Greco and Grecolaborativo</u> ^Material^ / Thrifted fabrics and recycled Polyfill stuffing ^Description^ / Soft sculpture based on original drawing by four-year-old boy.

- 7 -

- 8 -

- 1 -

1. — **Zid Zid** 2008, *Zid Zid Block Sets* ^{Design} / <u>Julie A. Klear</u>
^{Photography} / <u>Iann Collet</u> ^{Manufacturer} / <u>Zid Zid Kids</u> ^{Material} / Embroidered high quality
vinyl ^{Description} / Babies and toddlers can use these creative shapes to invent
secret worlds and beyond. Gold, white, lime, brown, red. Sizes range from 3 to
14 in. and 7 to 36 cm.

2. — 2008, *The Zid Zid Caravan Block Sets* ^{Design} / <u>Julie A. Klear</u>
^{Photography} / <u>Iann Collet</u> ^{Manufacturer} / <u>Zid Zid Kids</u> ^{Material} / Embroidered high quality
vinyl ^{Description} / Sizes range from 3 to 14 in. and 7 to 36 cm. Little caravan of a
camel, elephant, giraffe, bird and lion in blue, brown, orange, silver, gold.

3. — **Tas-ka** 2008, *Playhouses* ^{Design} / <u>Hester Worst, Jantien Baas</u>
^{Manufacturer} / <u>Tas-ka</u> ^{Material} / Cotton with foam rubber inner ^{Description} / Playhouses
for building cities or for use as big pillows..

- 3 -

- 2 -

12 / 13

- 4 -

- 5 -

- 6 -

4. — **The Toy Society** 2008, *Lucas. The little Guy*
Design / <u>Desirée Franco @ PAXandLOVE</u> Material / Recycled wool sweater, cotton fabric and felt Description / The Toy Society is a crafts project sharing love throughout the world by leaving handmade soft toys for people to take home.

5. — 2008, *Kokeshi doll* Design / <u>Noe Arata</u> (doubleufa)
Material / Fabric, Polyfill.

6. — 2008, *Toy Drop #28*, Surry Hills, Sydney, Australia
Design / <u>Bianca Brownlow</u> Material / Fleece, cotton, Polyfill, beads.

- 1 -

HERZENSART

1. — herzensart 2008, *Olaf Trehogger (Olaf the Tree-feller)
and Hrolf Kraki (Rolf the Crow)* Design / Sandra Monat
Photography / Sandra Monat Manufacturer / herzensart
Material / Diverse cotton fabrics, thread, fake fur, artificial
leather, leather, coconut buttons, Polyfill stuffing.

2. — 2007, *Paulina with a herzensart viking* Design / <u>Sandra</u> <u>Monat</u> Photography / <u>Bogi Bell</u> Manufacturer / <u>herzensart</u> Material / Diverse fabrics, thread, ribbon, Polyfill stuffing.

3. — 2008, *Erik Bloodaxe* Design / <u>Sandra Monat</u> Photography / <u>Sandra Monat</u> Manufacturer / <u>herzensart</u> Material / Fabrics, leather, artificial leather, fake fur, wool, felt, buttons, cord, woodstick, Polyfill.

4. — 2008, *DRAKKAR pillows* Design / <u>Sandra Monat</u> Photography / <u>Sandra Monat</u> Manufacturer / <u>herzensart</u> Material / Cord fabric, cotton fabric, felt, fleece, ribbon, thread.

- 2 -

- 3 -

- 4 -

herzensart was launched by artist Sandra Monat after a blue sheep found its way to her studio revealing brand new creative options:

"When I rescued a wooden sheep from a garbage bin in summer 2005, I did not know that this would change my life completely. I restored the sheep, gave her a new blue hair-do and named her Friederike! With this new muse at my side, I began playing with fabrics and threads, combining patterns and textures and making my first three-dimensional textile pieces. After I got some nice feedback from showing my creations to people, I felt encouraged to go on and developed my own designs for playful soft art toys, which I offered for sale."

Since that day, herzensart stands for playful and imaginative art toys, which address our inner child. The characters, which include friendly and naughty Vikings, wise knights, and cute guardian angels, are not merely decorative objects, but soulful personalities. Each meticulously crafted toy is handmade out of high quality material and pays careful attention to contemporary design.

1. — **herzensart** 2008, *Sea King* ^{Design} / <u>Sandra Monat</u>
^{Photography} / <u>Bogi Bell</u> ^{Manufacturer} / <u>herzensart</u> ^{Material} / Diverse
cotton fabrics, thread, Polyfill stuffing.

2. — 2008, *Playing with paper* ^{Design} / <u>Sandra Monat</u>
^{Photography} / <u>Bogi Bell</u> ^{Manufacturer} / <u>herzensart</u> ^{Material} / Papers,
scissors, glue ^{Description} / herzensart Viking designs turned
into paper.

- 1 -

- 2 -

3. — 2008, *herzensart Viking* ^{Design} / <u>Sandra Monat</u> ^{Photography} / <u>Sandra Monat</u> ^{Manufacturer} / <u>herzensart</u> ^{Material} / Diverse cotton fabrics, thread, ribbon, buttons, Polyfill stuffing.

4. — 2008, *Axe rattles for little vikings* ^{Design} / <u>Sandra Monat</u> ^{Photography} / <u>Sandra Monat</u> ^{Manufacturer} / <u>herzensart</u> ^{Material} / Cotton cord, terry cloth, rattle, stuffed with Polyfill.

5. — 2008, *Knights templar Hugo of Payens and his horse Charlotte* ^{Design} / Sandra Monat ^{Photography} / <u>Sandra Monat</u> ^{Manufacturer} / <u>herzensart</u> ^{Material} / Various new and recycled cotton fabrics, acrylic felt, thread, cord, wool, ribbons.

- 1 -

- 2 -

1. — **Joshua Ben Longo** 2008, *Monster Couch*
Design / Joshua Ben Longo   Photography / Longoland
Manufacturer / Longoland   Material / Felt fleece stuffing
Description / 7 ft. long, 3 ft. wide.

2. — 2006, *Macho*   Design / Joshua Ben Longo
Photography / Longoland   Manufacturer / Longoland.

3. — 2006, *Monster Skin Rug*   Design / Joshua Ben Longo
Photography / Longoland   Manufacturer / Longoland   Material / Wool
polymer clay   Description / Small: approx. 18 x 26in. Medium:
approx 36 x 50in. Large: approx 50 x 70in.

4. — 2008, *untitled*   Design / Joshua Ben Longo
Photography / Longoland   Manufacturer / Longoland   Material / Cotton
batting, felt, polymer clay, stuffing.

- 3 -

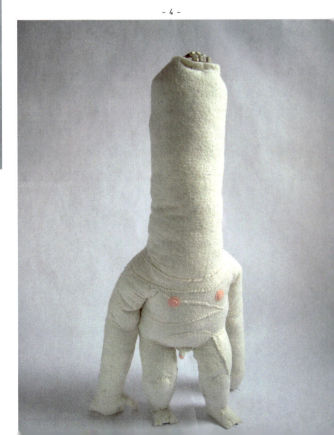

- 4 -

- 1 -

- 2 -

1. — **Smoodoos** 2008 *Smoodoos: Group picture*, Design / Janina Fey Manufacturer / just us and friends GmbH Material / Plush.

2. — **SewSew** 2008 *Rene the Straw-be-ret*, Design / Claire Walls Material / Embroidery silk, felt, plastic eyes.

3. — 2008 *The SewSew collection*, Design / Claire Walls Photography / Loz Ives, Emma Smart Material / Cotton, acrylic, felt, plastic eyes, embroidery thread.

- 3 -

- 4 -

- 4 -

4. — **woOberry** 2008, *Big Truck!* ^{Design} / <u>Wester Shermeta, Melissa Conroy</u> ^{Material} / Bamboo velour, silk organza and felt ^{Description} / A handmade plush truck based on a drawing by Wester at 22 months. It is 8 in. tall.

5. — 2008, *Lila* ^{Design} / <u>Lila Shermeta, Melissa Conroy</u> ^{Photography} / <u>Melissa Conroy</u> ^{Material} / Cotton velveteen, vintage cotton prints, silk organza, cotton yarn ^{Description} / A one-of-a-kind handmade doll inspired by a drawing done by Lila at age 6, 14 in. tall.

- 5 -

6. — 2008, *rOsemary & gEorge* ^{Design} / <u>Melissa Conroy</u> ^{Material} / Cotton velveteen, cotton prints & cotton yarn ^{Description} / Two handmade plush dolls, approximately 14 in. tall each.

7. — 2007, *Two Dads* ^{Design} / <u>Lila Shermeta , Melissa Conroy</u> ^{Material} / Cotton velveteen, cotton prints, plaid suiting, silk & cotton yarn ^{Description} / Two handmade plush dolls, 14 & 16 in. tall. Made by Melissa, inspired by Lila's drawings.

8. — 2007, *Brothers*, Red & Garney ^{Design} / <u>Lila Shermeta, Melissa Conroy</u> ^{Material} / Cotton velveteen, cotton prints, silk & cotton yarn ^{Description} / Two handmade plush dolls, inspired by Lila's drawings. They are both 14 in. tall.

- 6 - - 7 - - 8 -

- 1 -

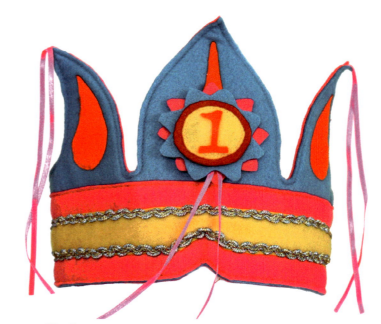

- 2 -

- 3 -

1. — **Birdy nam nam** 2008, *Plaid oehoe owl* ^{Design} / <u>Jopie Biesters</u> ^{Manufacturer} / <u>Birdy nam nam</u> ^{Material} / Felt, cotton ^{Description} / This owl is an item for the bed-time ritual and can open and close its eyes.

2. — 2007, *Birthdaycrown* ^{Design} / <u>Jopie Biesters</u> ^{Manufacturer} / <u>Birdy nam nam</u> ^{Material} / Felt ^{Description} / Colorful, adjustable and with four medals (Numbers 1 to 4) to celebrate the first four birthdays.

3. — 2007, *Birthday Medal* ^{Design} / <u>Jopie Biesters</u> ^{Manufacturer} / <u>Birdy nam nam</u> ^{Material} / Felt ^{Description} / A winners' medal, with a pin. Size 15 x 9 cm.

4. — **Judith Drews** 2008, *Miniatures* ^{Design} / <u>Judith Drews</u> ^{Material} / Fimo ^{Description} / Small things for small dolls.

5. — 2008, *Little Doll* ^{Design} / <u>Judith Drews</u> ^{Material} / Fimo ^{Description} / Match Box Doll.

- 4 -

- 5 -

6. **FriendsWithYou** — 2004, *The Malfis* ^{Design} / FriendsWithYou ^{Description} / Malfi, Super Malfi, Smiling Malfi, The Boy, The Burger Bunch, Muffin, Mr. TTT, Burger, Bumble Grump.

7. — 2002, *Poppings* ^{Design} / FriendsWithYou.

8. — 2002, *Albino Squid* ^{Design} / FriendsWithYou.

9. — 2008, *Rainbow TTT* ^{Design} / FriendsWithYou.

10. — 2002, *Red Flyer* ^{Design} / FriendsWithYou.

- 1 -

- 2 -

- 3 -

- 4 -

- 5 -

BRIO®

- 6 -

1. — **Active People** 2007, *Bilibo Pixel* ^{Design} / <u>Alex Hochstrasser</u> ^{Manufacturer} / <u>Active People</u> ^{Material} / Dice: TPR, Chips: ABS ^{Description} / Bilibo Pixel is a set of 36 chips in six colours and an elastic cube where the chips can be inserted to create custom colour dice. Bilibo Pixel encourages the discovery and invention of new games.

2. + 3. — 2005, *Babal* ^{Design} / <u>Alex Hochstrasser</u> ^{Manufacturer} / <u>Active People</u> ^{Material} / Polyurethane foam ^{Description} / Babal is a ball that is actually two balls. Together, big and small, soft and colourful, they open up endless possibilities. Babal appeals to many basic playing modes of children and stimulates their imagination.

4. — 2006, *Bilibo Mini* ^{Design} / <u>Alex Hochstrasser</u> ^{Manufacturer} / Active People ^{Material} / HD-PE.

5. — 2001, *Bilibo* ^{Design} / <u>Alex Hochstrasser</u> ^{Manufacturer} / <u>Active People</u> ^{Material} / HD-PE.

6. — **BRIO**, *Sorting Box* ^{Design} / <u>Brio</u> ^{Manufacturer} / <u>Brio AB</u> ^{Material} / Wood ^{Description} / A classic wooden toy where the child gets to learn about the most common shapes and work with hand/eye coordination.

7. — **Fillintheblanks** 2008, *Global Warning Toys*   Design / <u>Uçman Balaban</u>
Photography / <u>Maurizio Braggiotti</u>   Description / Global warming is a major problem in today's world. The project's main theme is not forgetting that drastic changes always start from a little wee bit of an idea. They are cute, weeby warning signs for our living spaces.

8. — **FriendsWithYou** 2007, *Good Wood Gang*   Design / <u>FriendsWithYou</u>
Material / Wood   Description / The Good Wood gang is an adventure into wooden toys; 500 limited edition.

- 1 -

1. — **Marcus Walters** 2008, *My First Alphabet*
Design / Marcus Walters   Material / 230 gsm Cyclus offset - 50 x
70 cm   Description / An A-Z originally created from collage and
reprinted on recycled stock.

2 - 4. — **MillerGoodman** 2008, *Shape*
Design / David Goodman, Zoe Miller   Manufacturer / MillerGoodman for TATE   Description / Spreads from the book.

- 2 -

- 3 -

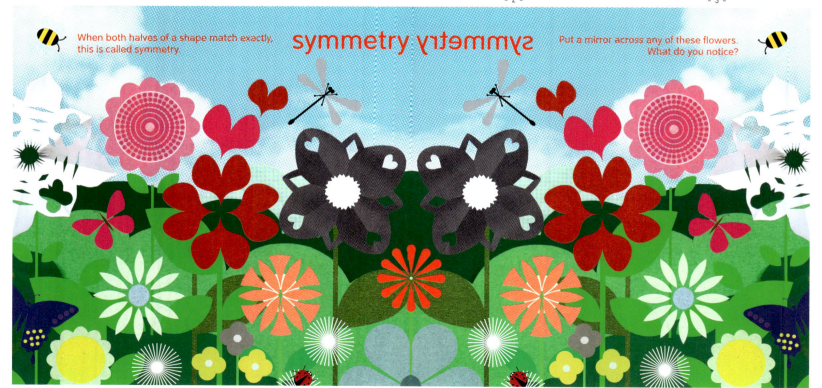

- 4 -

Binth 2009, *Binth Matching Game* Design / Binth Photography / Binth Manufacturer / Chronicle
Material / Recycled paper and boards Description / Binth's version of the classic memory game.

MillerGoodman 2008, *Shapemaker* Design / <u>David Goodman, Zoe Miller</u>
Manufacturer / <u>MillerGoodman</u> Material / Rubber, wood.

MillerGoodman 2008, *Shape* Design / David Goodman, Zoe Miller
Manufacturer / MillerGoodman for TATE.

↗ This lavish book, bursting with sparkling images and intriguing activities exploring the world of shape, gives children a fresh and informal introduction to both 2D and 3D shapes, as well as to concepts such as tessellation, symmetry and pattern. It celebrates the possibility of combining squares, triangles and circles or cubes, cylinders and cones.

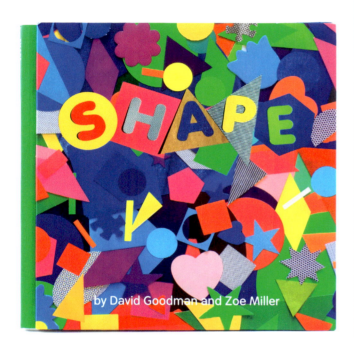

pyramid

– 2 –

– 1 –

– 3 –

– 4 –

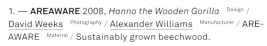

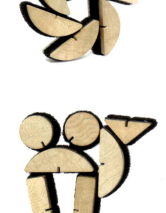

– 5 –

1. — **AREAWARE** 2008, *Hanno the Wooden Gorilla* Design / David Weeks Photography / Alexander Williams Manufacturer / AREAWARE Material / Sustainably grown beechwood.

2. — **Mini Spielzeug** 2008, *Mini Shop* Design / Lousy Animal by Stefan Marx.

3. — 2008, *Dog* Design / Mini.

4. — 2008, *Car* Design / Mini.

5. — **Active People**, *Sakol* Design / Jean-Maurice Varone Photography / Alex Hochstrasser Manufacturer / Active People Material / Natural wood, velcro Description / Sakol is a toy for hands, head and heart using only five basic shapes. The wooden blocks with velcro lining offer new, organic ways of constructing, and nuanced possibilities for expression. Sakol encourages motor skills, the power of abstract thought, the sense of touch, imagination and aesthetic sensitivity.

- 6 -

6. — **Brio** 2006, *Rechargeable 4WD Engine* ^{Design} / Brio ^{Photography} / Brio ^{Manufacturer} / Brio AB ^{Description} / Includes a back-up battery so kids don't have to stop playing while the unit is charging. With front headlights and manual stop and start button. Battery charger included.

7. — 2008, *Rock on* ^{Design} / Brio ^{Photography} / Brio ^{Manufacturer} / Brio AB ^{Material} / Wood.

8. — *Pull-along engine* ^{Design} / Brio ^{Photography} / Brio ^{Manufacturer} / Brio AB ^{Material} / Wood.

9. — 1953, *Large and small dachshund* ^{Design} / Brio ^{Photography} / Brio ^{Manufacturer} / Brio AB ^{Material} / Wood.

- 7 -

- 8 -

- 9 -

- 1 -

- 2 -

1. — **Salon Elfi Berlin** 2008, *ABC Pyramid* Design / Verena Schaetzlein Material / Silkscreen print on cardboard Description / 9 nested boxes, all sides have patterns or illustrations. They include an illustrated ABC, which functions in both English and German.

2. — 2008, *Paper theatre with props and finger puppets* Design / Verena Schaetzlein Material / Cardboard, heavy paper, handpainted lathed wood, cotton.

3. — 2007, *Bowling-set* Design / Verena Schaetzlein Material / Handpainted lathed wood, cotton Description / 9 wooden cones and one ball for long corridors or outdoor use. Comes in a cotton bag for carrying or storing

4. — 2007, *The Brick-Box* Design / Verena Schaetzlein Material / Handpainted lathed wood Description / 30 different wooden pieces in a cardboard-box to build your own dream-castle or refine your existing simple bricks.

- 3 -

- 4 -

- 5 -

- 6 -

- 7 -

- 8 -

- 9 -

5. — **Judith Drews** 2009, *Docteur Bobo* Design / éditions tourbillon Manufacturer / © éditions tourbillon Material / New material, polyurethane foam stuffing, polyester fibre.

6. — **Esthex** 2008, *Rocket Musicbox* Design / Esther Schuivens Photography / Rob Truijen Manufacturer / Esthex Material / Cotton.

7. — 2007, *Big Car cushion 'Handymanvan'* Design / Esther Schuivens Photography / Rob Truijen Manufacturer / Esthex Material / Cotton.

8. — 2007, *Handymanvan Car musicbox* Design / Esther Schuivens Photography / Rob Truijen Manufacturer / Esthex Material / Cotton.

9. — **Hikje Janneke Zantinge** 2008, *Little cranes* Design / Janneke Zantinge Material / Cardboard and string Description / These little cranes are made of cardboard and wrapped in cotton string, while the ball and wheels are wooden.

Clockwise from left — **Renate Müller** 1968-1974, *'Therapeutic Toy' Hippopotamus*, *'Therapeutic Toy' Cube*, *'Therapeutic Toy' Seal*, *'Therapeutic Toy' Bowling Pins with Ball*, *'Therapeutic Toy' Rhinoceros* ^{Design} / <u>Renate Müller</u> ^{Photography} / <u>Sherry Griffin for R 20th Century, New York</u> ^{Manufacturer} / <u>H. Josef Leven, Sonneberg, Germany</u> ^{Material} / Jute with leather detailing.

Michaela Tomišková 2008, *Children's ride-on monster with wheels* Design / Michaela Tomišková Material / Protctype made of laminate shell and painted using toy-friendly, non-toxic paints.

↗ Monster has an indefinable animal shape which is poking along the childhood world. Monster is an animal cross connection, which is defined as a connection between snail, bunny, sea monster and children's rocking horse. The toy's shape enables young children to ride on or to rock on it. There are fourteen wheels underneath the monster. There are also tender feed stops which prevent children from falling upon. It is easy for children to move forward on the toy.

Floris Hovers 2007, *ArcheToys: Cars* ᴰᵉˢⁱᵍⁿ / Floris Hovers
ᴹᵃⁿᵘᶠᵃᶜᵗᵘʳᵉʳ / Goods ᴾʰᵒᵗᵒᵍʳᵃᵖʰʸ / Goods ᴹᵃᵗᵉʳⁱᵃˡ / Metal
ᴰᵉˢᶜʳⁱᵖᵗⁱᵒⁿ / These model cars by Dutch designer Floris Hovers are
instantly recognisable. Hovers assembles what he calls ArcheToys, archetypes of familiar motorised vehicles, with basic
factory-made metal parts. The young designer can create a
three-dimensional impression of an ambulance, a fire truck or
a double decker bus with few elements, but enough imagination to make anyone smile with surprise.

Jesco von Puttkamer 2008, *Alu objects* ^{Design} / <u>Jesco von Puttkamer</u> ^{Material} / 1 mm iron sheeting, 1mm, mortised, transparent varnish.

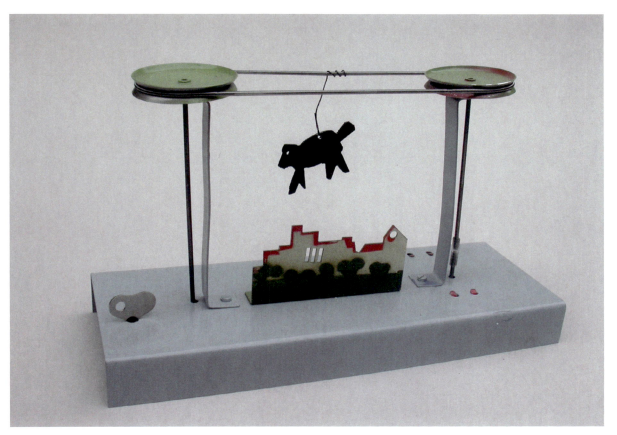

- 1 -

1. — **PastelToys** 2007, *Baby Hanging Swing* Design / PastelToys Manufacturer / PastelToys Material / Wood, MDF.

2. — 2003, *Elephant on Wheels* Design / Pastel-Toys Manufacturer / PastelToys Material / Wood, MDF.

3. — 2003, *Rabbit on Wheels* Design / Pastel-Toys Manufacturer / PastelToys Material / Wood, MDF.

4. — 2003, *Giraffe on Wheels* Design / Pastel-Toys Manufacturer / PastelToys Material / Wood, MDF.

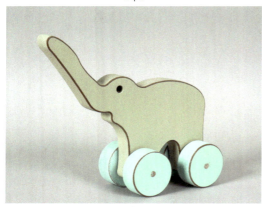

- 2 -

- 3 -

5. — 2004, *Maya Doll Cradle* Design / Pastel-Toys Manufacturer / PastelToys Material / Wood, MDF.

6. — 2006, *Small Rocking Horse* Design / PastelToys Manufacturer / PastelToys Material / Wood, MDF.

7. — 2004, *Max Truck with Blocks Trailer* Design / PastelToys Manufacturer / Pastel-Toys Material / Wood, MDF.

- 4 -

- 5 -

- 6 -

- 7 -

- 8 -

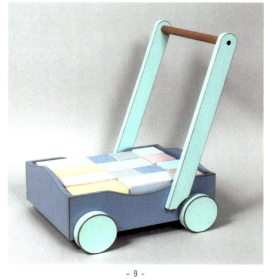

- 9 -

- 10 -

- 11 -

- 11 -

8. — **PastelToys** 2007, *Bimba Mixie*
Design / PastelToys Material / Wood, MDF.

9. — 2004, *Micki Walker with Blocks*
Design / PastelToys Material / Wood, MDF.

10. — **Tas-ka** 2008, *Tricycle* Design / <u>Hester
Worst, Jantien Baas</u> Material / Beechwood,
cotton.

11. — **Gavin Coultrip** 2006, *Brush Beauty* Design / <u>Gavin Coultrip</u> Photography / <u>Gareth
Hacker</u> Material / Birch, pine, coco.

Wishbone Design Studio 2007, *Wishbone Bike: two-wheel and three-weel configuration* ^{Design} / <u>Richard Latham</u> ^{Photography} / <u>Mark Weakley</u> ^{Manufacturer} / <u>Wishbone Design Studio</u> ^{Material} / Plantation-sourced birch plywood, 60% post-consumer recycled plastic, rubber, aluminium and steel.

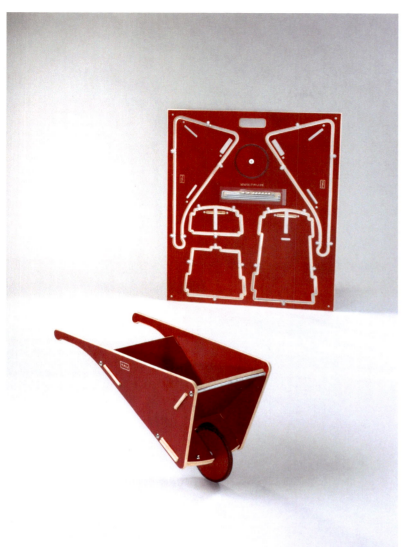

Clockwise from top — **Tau® KidsProducts** 2006, *Wheelbarrow, Toboggan* Design / Jörn Alexander Stelzner Photography / Yvonne Dickopf Material / Plywood with a birch veneer, coated with a coloured film. The material is firm and flexible at the same time. The visible veneer layers are watertight, glued and protected by natural oils and waxes. The furniture is made with a high percentage of solid wood. All furniture from Tau is made according to the high standards of DIN EN 71.

2007, *Mia and Gilma with Tau seesaw* Photography / Rene Staebler

2006, *SeeSaw* Design / Jörn Alexander Stelzner Photography / Anna Britz Description / The Tau PuzzleFurniture is delivered as a single sheet of plywood. It holds all the parts you need to put together the furniture. The puzzle elements are taken out of the plate, put together and secured with a few screws. The production run is very limited.

Arounna Khounnoraj | bloesemkids 2008,
Collage moveable figure Design / Arounna
Khounnoraj, bookhou Photography / Arounna
Khounnoraj Material / Magazines, paper, glue,
brass fasteners.

AROUNNA KHOUNNORAJ

- 1 -

1. — 2008, *Project: Puppet* Design / Arounna Khounnoraj Photography / Arounna Khounnoraj Material / Glass bottle, plaster bandages, newspaper, water, paint.

This is Old School, been-around-since-the-beginning-of-time design. Got some cardboard, a skein of yarn, a mateless cufflink? Designer and artist Arounna Khounnoraj of Ontario, Canada's BloesemKids uses the abandoned and rescued scraps of the domestic realm to make her work and to put her kids to work. She cooked up her Found Object Mobile with such simple ingredients as morsels of metal and wood, wilted string and a few pert buttons. She pasted images cut from magazines together with glue to make 2D figures that were endowed with movable joints - thanks to a little prosthetic surgery with brass fasteners.

'The materials that I choose are things that can be commonly found in your home,' says Khounnoraj, who makes textiles and artwork that explore sculpture, drawing and printmaking, pattern and image, along with the kids' objects. 'I enjoy reusing found materials and materials that have a history or taking materials that once had a different purpose and reassigning them with a new purpose for an art project. Also, it's fun to come up with a project for something I already have, the things already available in our environment or the things we collect, instead of searching for a new material or relying solely on things that we need to buy.'

Khounnoraj received her education at the Ontario College of Art, a B.F.A from the Nova Scotia College of Art and Design and an M.F.A from the University of Waterloo. Having taught children for several years, she began making objects for children, including textiles, toys, clothing and modified art projects after she had her first child. Today, she has two. Together they make puppets from glass bottles, plaster bandages, newsprint, water and paint or generate colourful canvases by painting with watercolours over marks made with wax crayons.

Her Scribble Garden project was inspired by doodles that Khounnoraj makes in her sketchbooks and uses to create screen-printed textiles in her design studio. Drawing with ink appeals to her because it has a liquid flow and uncontrolled quality that can't be gotten from a pencil or marker. The Scribble Garden toolkit includes paper, Indian ink, brushes, scissors and a glue stick to design a collage that pulls together the wild character of the scribbles to create a coherent 'drawing'. 'Everybody can scribble,' the artist insists. 'It's fun and it can be beautiful.'

2 - 3. — 2008, *Project: Frame Art* Design / Arounna Khounnoraj, bookhou Photography / Arounna Khounnoraj Material / Wood frame, scrap wood, found objects, hot glue, paint, wire Description / Abstract frame art piece using found materials and wood.

- 2 -

- 3 -

- 4 -

The objects she makes for kids, however, tend to be an extension of the things she is making anyway for herself or other adults, the difference being that the children's projects are usually more accessible, faster and easier to fabricate. The craft is scaled down but always consists of activities that an adult would find just as exciting – and challenging. 'The projects tend to be process-based rather than skill-based,' Khounnoraj explains. 'They take advantage of anybody's ability to make marks, but still leave room for personal gestures and directions. There is a link between the two, a similar sensibility; my philosophy is that there shouldn't be much of a distinction between things for children and things for adults.'

Arounna Khounnoraj 2008, *Project: Puppet*
Design / Arounna Khounnoraj   Photography / Arounna Khounnoraj   Material / Glass bottle, plaster bandages, newspaper, water, paint.

- 1 -

1. — 2008, *Project: Scribble Garden* Design / <u>Arounna Khoun-noraj</u> Photography / <u>Arounna Khounnoraj</u> Material / Paper, Indian ink, brush, scissors, gluestick.

2 + 3. — 2008, *Found Object Mobile* Design / <u>Arounna Khoun-noraj</u> Photography / <u>Arounna Khounnoraj</u> Material / Wood, string, metal, buttons.

- 2 -

- 3 -

4 + 5. — 2008, *Project: Scribble Garden* Design / <u>Arounna Khounnoraj</u> Photography / <u>Arounna Khounnoraj</u> Material / Paper, Indian ink, brush, scissors, gluestick.

- 4 -

- 5 -

↗ "Crea il tuo spazio" ("create your own space") is an exhibition/workshop realised during the Salone del Mobile 2007, at Rotonda della Besana. "Crea il tuo spazio" takes place along 40 metres of both sides of the Rotonda's curved arcade, and introduces white cardboard play elements which take shape and meaning through children's interaction, encouraging creativity and teamwork. The exhibition was divided into three areas: 1 - Micro città: 50 white cardboard polyhedral houses, placed together to form a miniature city. Children can inhabit the homes and reassemble the urban landscape experimenting with possible layouts: streets, rows, asymmetry. 2 - Cards: 2000 white cardboard cards form three-dimensional walls and fantasy objects that changes shape through interaction and play. 3 - Installation of white cardboard house1 customised by children and artists.

Opposite page — **nume** 2006, *vorrei il tetto blu con le stelline d'oro* ^{Design} / nume | design for children ^{Photography} / Paolo Bramati ^{Material} / Build-it-yourself playhouse made of white cardboard that children can decorate and customize. Size: 90x100x117 cm.

This page — 2007, *crea il tuo spazio* ^{Design} / nume | design for children ^{Photography} / Andrea Ferrari ^{Additional credits} / Curator: Tanja Solci. Project: Elisa Ossino, Raffaella Ossino, Sabien Devriendt. Patronaged by the Milan City Council, Department of Identity. ^{Material} / White cardboard (polyhedral house, cards and house1) Wool, carded wool, felt, cotton, velvet, clay, paper, card, wood, string, straw, leaves, cork, canvass, crayons, felt-tips, paints.

- 1 -

- 3 -

- 4 -

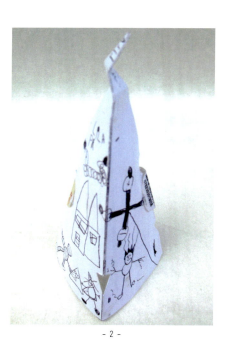

- 2 -

48 / 49

- 5 -

– 6 –

– 7 –

1. — **woOberry** 2008, *Monster* ^{Design} / <u>Lila Shermeta</u> ^{Photography} / <u>Melissa Conroy</u> ^{Material} / Cardboard box, the back of a large drawing pad, markers, fabric scraps ^{Description} / A monster that was made to keep the bad guys away at night.

2. — 2008, *Haunted House* ^{Design} / <u>Lila Shermeta</u> ^{Material} / Bristol board, ballpoint pen & drafting darts ^{Description} / This haunted house was made by Lila at age 6 to celebrate trick or treating with friends.

3. — 2008, *Instrument* ^{Design} / <u>Lila Shermeta</u> ^{Material} / Wooden stool, rubber band, baby wipes, elastic trimming, crayons ^{Description} / An instrument to be plucked like a guitar.

The baby wipes were twisted together into a flower with some left over trimming from our dolls' dresses. The flower was attached to the legs of the upside down stool with rubber bands to create the proper tension for plucking. Lila did this project on her own at age 6.

4 - 7. — **Ann Wood** 2008, *Castle* ^{Design} / <u>Ann Wood</u> ^{Photography} / <u>Ann Wood</u> ^{Material} / Discarded cardboard boxes.

8. — 2008, *Shipwreck* ^{Design} / <u>Ann Wood</u> ^{Photography} / <u>Ann Wood</u> ^{Material} / Paper maché, vintage and antique lace and garments.

– 8 –

- 1 -

- 2 -

1. — **Kidsonroof** 2006, *MobileHome*, Design / Ilya Yashkin Material / Recycled corrugated cardboard Description / Mobile-Home is for boys and girls. A little house with 8 rooms, an attick and spyholes. The first take-away house for kids on the move. To paint and decorate – for all favourite figurines.

2. — **cardboardesign** 2004, *the Playhouse*, Design / Paul Martin Photography / Paul Martin Manufacturer / cardboardesign Material / Cardboard.

3. — 2004, *the Fort / Castle*, Design / Paul Martin Photography / Paul Martin Manufacturer / cardboardesign Material / Cardboard.

- 3 -

Villa Carton 2008, *Cardboard Dollhouse*
Design / <u>Villa Carton</u>   Manufacturer / <u>Villa Car-</u>
<u>ton</u>   Material / Cardboard   Description / The doll-
house is made of white cardboard and can
be decorated as you wish. Its interior is
a colouring page. The dollhouse is 59 cm
high, 40 cm deep and 45 cm wide and can
only be constructed once.

Top — **Kleine Burgen** 2007-2009, *Little castles* Design / Olaf Hoffmann
Material / Wood, acrylic, div.

Bottom — **Cubeecraft** 2008, *Cubeecraft Originals* Design / Christopher Beaumont and others Photography / Chris and Marisa Material / Digital prints on cardboard Description / Papercraft toys Additional credits / From l. to r.: 'poprockboy' by Harlancore, 'Kakuula' - collaboration Chent / Cubeecraft, 'Ernie from the Black Lagoon' by Glen Brogan and 'thehermitdesign' by Arthur.

3 + 4. — **Carton Chic** 2007, *Archi-Television Reversible cardboard theatre* Manufacturer / Carton Chic Material / Recycled and recyclable cardboard Description / This reversible theatre shows a flat screen on a stand. Pop out the TV screen and your child can put on endless performances. Reverse the theater and it's a play kitchen. Easy to assemble, and very stable, it is printed on both sides.

5 - 7. — 2007, *Archi Maison Garage, L'archi-maison2* Design / Clara Courtaigne Photography / Gaetan Bernard Manufacturer / Carton Chic Material / Ecological cardboard, 100% pulp, comes from certified PEFC/FSC forest.

8. — 2008, *Archi Masion Cloud Little Fashion Gallery* Manufacturer / Carton Chic Material / Ecological cardboard, 100% pulp, comes from certified PEFC et FSC forest.

- 3 -

- 4 -

- 5 -

- 8 -

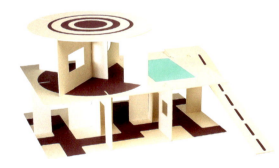

- 6 -

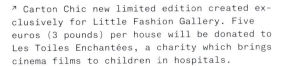

↗ Carton Chic new limited edition created exclusively for Little Fashion Gallery. Five euros (3 pounds) per house will be donated to Les Toiles Enchantées, a charity which brings cinema films to children in hospitals.

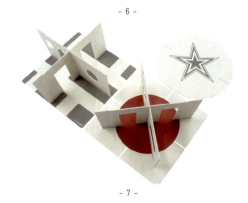

- 7 -

Kristian Kutschera 2008, *Cardboard-knight kit* Design / Kristian Kutschera Photography / bürokutschera Material / 2 mm grey cardboard and cardboard roll Description / The cardboard rolls can hold endless variations of attached cutouts.

- 1 -

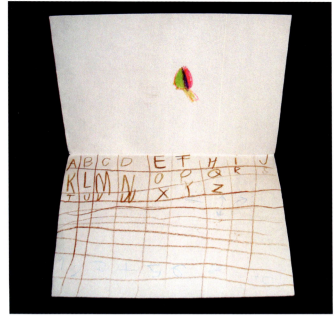

- 2 -

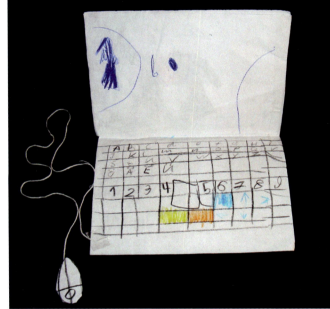

- 3 -

- 5 -

1 - 4. — **Hendrik Hellige** 2008, *KidsLaptop* ^{Design} / Mia Lova Korr ^{Photography} / Hendrik Hellige ^{Material} / Paper.

5. — 2008, *KidsMask* ^{Design} / Hendrik Hellige ^{Photography} / Hendrik Hellige ^{Material} / Paper.

6. — **Hans Baltzer** 2008, *Study on hair* ^{Design} / Emilie Baltzer ^{Material} / Pencil on paper.

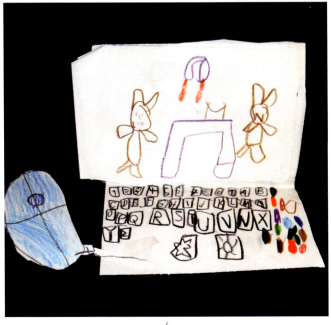

- 4 -

- 6 -

1. — **LULA** 2008, *Vintage Toys*   Design / <u>Elisabeth Dunker</u>
Description / A colloboration between bloggers Fine Little Day
and Reference Library for an exhibit.

2. — 2008, *Circus City*   Design / <u>Elisabeth Dunker</u>
Photography / <u>Elisabeth Dunker</u>   Material / Junk.

↗ Gothenburg-based Elisabeth Dunker crosses the borders between design, illustration, styling and photography. She founded
the design studio, which she runs together
with Camilla Engman, in 2008 after deciding
"that a mutual project or two was simply not
enough." Her illustrations and graphic designs embellish bedclothes, wallpaper, posters and magazine layouts.

3. — 2008, *Circus City* Design / Elisabeth Dunker
Photography / Elisabeth Dunker Material / Junk
Description / Reportage for Mama magazine.

4. — 2008, *Circus City* Design / Elisabeth Dunker
Photography / Elisabeth Dunker Material / Junk
Description / Report for Mama magazine.

5. — 2008, *Doll Houses* Design / Elisabeth Dunker
Photography / Elisabeth Dunker Assistant / Tovalisa
Description / Report for Petit Magazine.

- 1 -

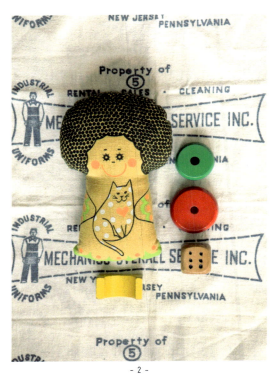

- 2 -

1. — **LULA** 2007, *Circus City*   ^{Design} / <u>Elisabeth Dunker</u>
^{Material} / Junk.

2. — 2008, *Vintage Toys*   ^{Design} / <u>Elisabeth Dunker</u>   ^{Material} /
Vintage Toys   ^{Photography} / <u>Elisabeth Dunker</u>   ^{Description} / A col-
loboration between bloggers Fine Little Day and Reference
Library for an exhibit / www.kioskkiosk.com.

3. — 2007, *Circus City*   ^{Design} / <u>Elisabeth Dunker</u>.

- 3 -

– 4 –

– 5 –

– 6 –

– 7 –

– 8 –

4 + 5. — LULA 2007, *Circus City*   Design / Elisabeth Dunker   Material / Junk.

6 - 8. — 2008, *Vintage Toys*   Design / Elisabeth Dunker   Material / Vintage Toys
Photography / Elisabeth Dunker   Description / A colloboration between bloggers Fine
Little Day and Reference Library for an exhibit / www.kioskkiosk.com.

PKNTS 2008, *Alle meine Klänge (All my sounds)*
Photography / Andreas Velten   Material / Polyurethane.

↗ 'AMK' is a modular sound toy for preschool children. In interaction with the computer, single sounds and entire sets can be transferred to sound blocks called 'Klangbausteine'(sound modules). The children can independently play and combine the sounds by plugging these blocks together. Only one sound per block and age-based limited possibilities of sound modification afford a basic game and offer the children an orientation within its own system. The main focus of 'AMK' is the self-contained play with sounds on the 'Klangbausteinen' without screen and computer.

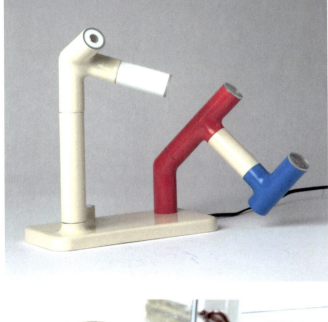

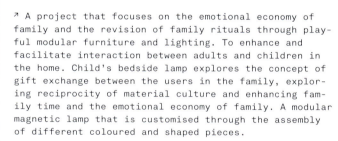

Paul Blease 2008, *Combinations of Magnetic Lamp*
Design / Paul Blease   Photography / Paul Blease   Material / Powder coated aluminium.

↗ A project that focuses on the emotional economy of family and the revision of family rituals through playful modular furniture and lighting. To enhance and facilitate interaction between adults and children in the home. Child's bedside lamp explores the concept of gift exchange between the users in the family, exploring reciprocity of material culture and enhancing family time and the emotional economy of family. A modular magnetic lamp that is customised through the assembly of different coloured and shaped pieces.

- 1 -

1. — **Lizette Greco** 2006, *2-Grin Robot*
Design / <u>Lizette Greco and Grecolaborativo</u>
Material / Thrifted fabrics and recycled Polyfill
stuffing   Description / Soft robot based on original
drawing by five-year-old boy.

2. — 2001, *Wild Thing*   Design / <u>Lizette Greco and
Grecolaborativo</u>   Photography / <u>Robert Greco</u>
Material / Fake fur and thrifted fabrics   Description /
Wild Thing was a costume made for a child for
Halloween 2001. It was inspired by Maurice
Sendak's *"Where The Wild Things Are"*, which
was the child's favourite book at the time.

- 2 -

3. — **Lizette Greco** 2007, *Dachskuh* Design / Lizette Greco and Grecolaborativo Photography / Robert Greco Material / Thrifted fabrics and recycled Polyfill stuffing Description / Soft sculpture based on original drawing by eight-year-old girl.

4. — 2007, *Mr. Cottontail* Design / Lizette Greco and Grecolaborativo Photography / Robert Greco Material / Thrifted fabrics and recycled Polyfill stuffing Description / Soft sculpture based on original drawing by seven-year-old boy.

5. — 2006, *Taxi* Design / Lizette Greco and Grecolaborativo Photography / Lizette Greco Material / Thrifted and recycled fabrics, recycled Polyfill stuffing Description / Soft toy based on original drawing by eight-year-old girl.

PLAYGROUNDS

Children can turn any ground that they occupy into their own playground since they interact naturally with their environment. So what exactly defines a playground? Technically speaking it is an enclosed space with swings, monkey bars and sandboxes where no dogs are allowed. In a broader sense, yet more specifically, a playground is a place where children learn about their skills and limitations. This basically means that every kindergarten and every school is a 'playground' as well. Albeit these so-called playgrounds have extended functions where there are stricter rules and ways of playing, a stronger need to act within social hierarchies and of course educators who guide the children. But basically they remain those essential environments where children learn the most about life and where they develop their personalities.

> This understanding in mind, why are there still so many playgrounds, schools and kindergartens that are rather grey and boring, if not daunting places? Don't worry; there is improvement on the horizon. In recent years a significant number of innovative projects have proven that there is still considerable room for improvement. This chapter introduces a selection of these improvements, ranging from interior designs for kindergartens and schools, to architectural projects, to installations and the re-design of public spaces. These examples are colourful, adventurous and leave enough space for a child's imagination.

The way children perceive the world and 'design' it for their own purpose has always been an essential inspiration for street and urban artists. Currently more and more artists propose that people actively participate in exhibitions and events rather than just having them watch from a distance. FriendsWithYou's installations/playgrounds allow and encourage kids and adults to explore a different, happy, and positive world. Once you actively take part in something, you see it in an entirely new light. Baupiloten have realised a project where architectural students worked for kindergartens and schools, with school children who took on the the role of their clients and also had a say in the design process. As a result, the children who were involved were taken more seriously and also improved in school, which is ultimately the most important reason for changing the learning environment. Dutch design and engineering bureau Carve focuses on the planning and development of public space, particularly for use by children and young people. They share similar positive experiences, although they choose to take a less direct approach: 'Of course we use children's input. When designing with kids, the outcome of their participation can vary depending on the techniques, briefing and coaching. Therefore, we find it more interesting to let kids talk or write, instead of letting them make DIY models from toilet paper rolls with a predictive outcome. In general, 95% of the kids have very conventional ideas but the other 5% are very inspiring.'

> PLAYGROUNDS examines how different countries have different needs and concepts about education, schools and kindergartens. While in one particular country it's all about very basic installations, in other countries the latest technical developments and theories are being discussed. But no matter how vastly the actual concepts may differ in size, function and detail, all these playgrounds, kindergartens and schools are places and spaces that provide an environment where education functions as the most essential safeguard against intolerance and the lack of courage.

2

Dorte Mandrup Arkitekter 2005, *Day-care centre in Skanderborggade*
Design / Dorte Mandrup Arkitekter   Photography / Jens Markus Lindhe.

↗ New Building. Situated within the Skanderborggade/Krausesvej block, the site is surrounded by 5-storey buildings and a narrow inner courtyard with little to almost no daylight. The zoning regulations for the site required the new day-care to be a maximum of one-storey, while the daycare needed an outdoor space almost equal to that of the actual building area. The design therefore, maximizes the sites daylighting and challenges the zoning regulations by placing the outdoor play area on the roof of the day-care centre and cutting light wells into the various indoor spaces. The formal arrangement of the building is composed of two folding planes which extend to the boundaries of the site. The lower plane forms a new ground covering the contaminated soil, and the upper plane forms the roof and outdoor play area. Melded together by a large fold, the slope follows the path of the summer sun from the northeast to the northwest offering the best sun exposure throughout the site. Underneath, a forest of columns fills an unheated space used during wet weather.

BTU Cottbus, Lehrstuhl Plastisches Gestalten *2008*, kinderSPIELgarten ^{Credits} / Linda Bley, Stefan Schreck, Tania Coelho, Prof. Jo Achermann, Gert Bendel, Karsten Meyer ^{Photography} / Lehrstuhl Plastisches Gestalten BTU Cottbus.

<u>CARVE</u>

In the world of skateboarding, to «carve» is to navigate around obstacles by leaning toeside or heelside. Carve also is the name given to the Amsterdam design and engineering office founded in 1997 by designer E.ger Blitz and civil designer and engineer Mark van der Eng that focuses on the planning and development of public space for young people. As former professional skateboarders, Blitz and van der Eng wanted to build the skateparks they had always wanted to skate in, but which they never were able to find. Since skateparks are often an integral part of playgrounds, they began to plan playgrounds as well. During the course of the past 11 years, however, Carve has grown into a multidisciplinary company that embraces everything from industrial design to landscape architecture.

Carve's play towers are part of the redesign of the Columbusplein square in an area of Amsterdam currently in the throes of revitalisation. Asphalt connects the two sides of the square, the surface of which is perfectly suited for skating, rollerblading and biking. Five-metre-wide sidewalks hem the yard and serve as an unobtru-

sive barrier that prevents kids from running into adjacent streets – without the interruption of fencing. Carve designed all of the street furniture, playground equipment and ball catchers, as well as a small building for the square's caretaker.

Wall-holla is a multifunctional play structure that Carve originally designed as part of a schoolyard, but which has become a stand-alone «playground product» that has been used in several projects. It includes a football field, a climbing facility and enough equipment for more than 60 children to play simultaneously despite limited space. Its vertical structure unites several functions that appeal to various age groups, including a crawl-through maze, a climbing wall and a lounging landscape. Because it's a modular system, Wall-holla can be constructed in different sizes and configurations and can even be extended to include a football goal, slides or fireman poles. The structure consists of

Carve 2007, *Playtowers* ^{Design} / <u>Carve</u> ^{Photography} / <u>Elger</u> <u>Blitz</u> ^{Manufacturer} / <u>Carve</u> ^{Material} / Coated steel, stainless steel, EPDM rubber, polyferro rope ^{Description} / Custom built playtowers, part of a landscape and playground. Design for Columbusplein, Amsterdam.

slender, undulating ribbons made from alternating sections of soft EPDM rubber, rope mesh and an open grid with the purpose of encouraging children 'to sit, walk, hang, swing, slide, run, jump, vault and hide.' According to the designers, who watched in surprise as the kids – anchored by the rippling structure – invented even more games than they had ever dreamed possible, 'The structure stimulates the sense of adventure and creativity.'

'Inspiration can come from a detail on a cell phone or interesting architecture. We love forms that are scateable and that can take on a variety of functions,' explains Carve product engineer Lucas Beukers. 'The ultimate form is a playable area that isn't recognised as such anymore; its form attracts users. In general, anything and everything can become a playable sculpture.'

Carve 2005, *Wall-holla* Design / Carve Photography / Milan van der Storm
Manufacturer / Metaplus (Benelux), Playpoint Singapore (Asia), Carve (all other countries
Material / Coated steel, EPDM rubber, polyferro rope Description / Multi-purpose playwall.

- 1 -

1 + 2 — **Medium** 2002, *Daupeney School Playground*, ^{Design}
/ Kinnear Landscape Architects ^{Description} / Daubeney School
playground, Kinnear Landscape Architects and artist Hattie Coppard. London, 2002. Part of the Hackney Wick Public
Art Programme. Sponsored by Renaisi and Hackney Learning Partnerships. Project landscape architect, Jake Ford.

- 2 -

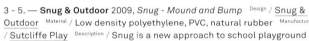

- 3 -

3 - 5. — **Snug & Outdoor** 2009, *Snug - Mound and Bump* Design / Snug & Outdoor Material / Low density polyethylene, PVC, natural rubber Manufacturer / Sutcliffe Play Description / Snug is a new approach to school playground equipment. Consisting of 9 modular objects that children can combine to create their own dynamic landscapes.

- 4 -

- 5 -

6. — **Snug & Outdoor** 2000, *Experimental Playground*, Daubeny School Design / Snug & Outdoor Additional credits / Landscape architect - Lynne Kinnear Description / This playground design has transformed a bleak chaotic playground into a sociable and playful environment. The playground incorporates many unique features including: rotating platforms, a forest of poles, and a giant zebra Crossing. There is also a hill, illuminated boulders and oversized mobile planters. All of this make a flexible, playful space which is also practical for the needs of the school.

- 6 -

Snug & Outdoor 2009, *Snug - Mound and Bump.*

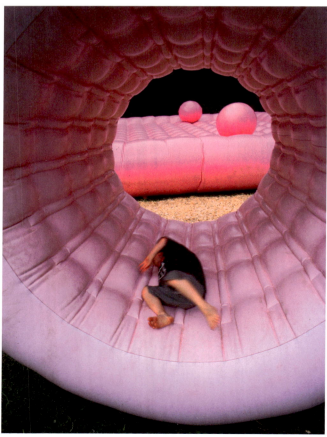

Topotek 1 2004, *Temporary Playground*
Design / <u>Topotek 1</u>   Photography / <u>Hanns Joosten</u>
Manufacturer / Airkraft GmbH   Material / Coated pink-coloured polyester fabric inflatable objects
Description / Installation at State Garden Show Wolfsburg 2004.

78 / 79

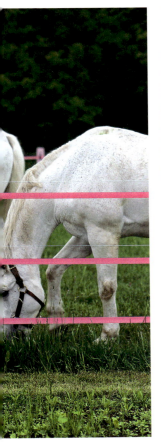

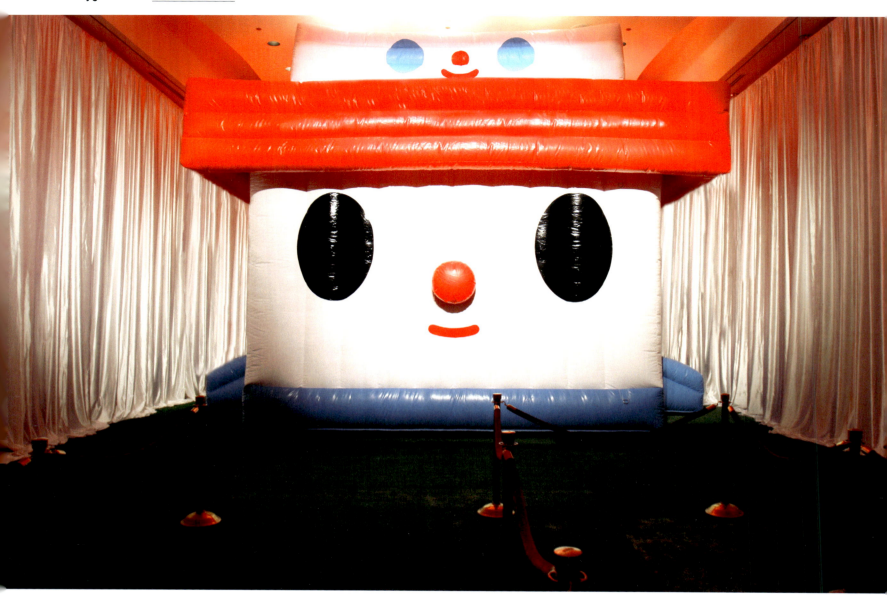

Top — **FriendsWithYou** 2008, *Fun House* ^{Design} / <u>FriendsWithYou</u> ^{Photography} / Hew Burney ^{Material} / 7 & 13 oz PVC Coated rip-stop nylon w/ digital print and custom paint ^{Description} / Fun House was designed as an interactive experience for adults and children.

Bottom — **FriendsWithYou** 2008, *Wish Come True Miami – Hexagone Art Show* ^{Design} / <u>FriendsWithYou</u>.

FriendsWithYou 2006, *Rainbow Valley.*

FRIENDSWITHYOU

Miami-based FriendsWithYou, aka Sam Borkson and Arturo Sandoval III, are the vanguards of the underground toy movement.

Originally the FriendsWithYou characters ventured into the world as hand-sewn plush dolls to provide magic and mayhem for their owners; now they have expanded to modular wooden toys, public art installations, motion pictures and more. This artist group was created with one basic concept in mind and that is to become friends with you: "The friends have magic powers never seen before, and are improving lives one person at a time. Share your wishes and desires with your new friends and watch, as everything you ever dreamed of becomes reality! Welcome friends into your heart and home and start living better TODAY!"

To stimulate a visitor's inner child through interplay, they recently created an immersive exhibition featuring, among other creature creations, a giant anthropomorphic bounce house that premiered at Art Basel Miami in 2008. This is something that is definitely not for spectators only, but is geared at being "an experience that will engage all aspects of the body and mind, providing for a euphoric art experience."

FriendsWithYou 2008, *Funhouse@ Scope Art Fair*
Design / FriendsWithYou.

↗ Café BooBah is a café specifically designed for children, their families and friends. The chairs and tables are low enough for kids of any age to feel comfortable and half of the space is devoted to a play area where every surface becomes a place for play and interactions. The Lego lounge has a view of the garden and consists of Lego boards covering the walls from floor to ceiling so children can build with or against gravity; everything a child builds becomes an integral part of the play space architecture until a new construction is made by someone else. There is a huge floor to ceiling abacus that also acts as a screening device, a chalkboard wall, a magnetic wall, and a wall for drawing on with crayons. The flooring is colourful and soft enough to cushion a child's fall and there are numerous built in benches and cubbies filled with toys. There are also lots of large soft, coloured geometric shapes with which kids can build their own environments to play in and on. The backyard garden has live bamboo, flowers, trees, a big sandbox and a two storey play house with lots of fun features. Parents and caregivers are perhaps Café BooBah's most enthusiastic patrons. It is one restaurant where adults can relax with a cup of coffee or light meal while their kids are free to run around and entertain themselves as they wish. Café BooBah serves delicious organic food including many of children's favourite treats like macaroni & (no) cheese, (tofu) hotdogs and peanut butter and jelly sandwiches.

I-Beam Design + Architecture, *Cafe BooBah* Design / Vrinda Khanna with I-Beam
Photography / Silke Mayer Additional credits / Cafe Concept: Lena Seow, Elizabeth Pressman.
Cafe Owner: Lena Seow. Garden Design and Construction: Lena Seow, Richard Seow.
Architecture and design: Lena Seow, Vrinda Khanna in collaboration with Suzan Wines.

TJEP.

Tjep. is an Amsterdam-based design studio that was founded by Frank Tjepkema and Janneke Hooymans. They work in diverse fields with a small team of highly motivated designers. This means anything from a sofa made out of a nest of giant rubber branches to complete interiors and identities for restaurants, schools and shops. Selected to design a restaurant that would appeal to both adults and children and would avoid the worn tropes of the family eatery, Tjep. created the first Praq in Amersfoort which was followed by an additional location in 2008. The environment is dictated by its massive farm-style roof with thick exposed wooden beams. The designers created elements that served as both decorative objects and functional pieces: A table is also a window, a bus or a kitchen. A six-metre installation anchors the centre of the room, resembling a colourful game of Connect Four, while providing a satisfying contrast to the handcrafted architectural elements.

Tjep. 2008, *Praq Amersfoort* Design / Tjep. Photography / Tjep.
Additional credits / Frank Tjepkema, Janneke Hooymans, Tina Stieger, Leonie Janssen, Bertrand Gravier, Camille Cortet.

Emily Gobeille & Theodore Watson 2007, *Funky Forest: An Interactive Ecosystem* Design / Emily Gobeille & Theodore Watson Photography / Emily Gobeille & Theodore Watson Material / Computer visionbased interactive environment. Made with openFrameworks.

↗ Funky Forest is a wild and crazy ecosystem where the resources influence the environment. Streams of water flowing on the floor can be diverted to make the different parts of the forest grow. If a tree does not receive enough water it withers away but by pressing one's body into the forest it is possible to create new trees based on one's shape and character. By exploring and playing, one discovers that the environment is inhabited by sonic life forms who depend on a thriving ecosystem to survive.

Kashiwa Sato 2004 - 2007, *Fuji Kindergarten*
Design / Kashiwa Sato   Photography / Mikiya Sato
Additional credits / Creative director: Kashiwa Sato.
Art Director: Kashiwa Sato.
Graphic Designer: Ko Ishikawa.
Architect: Takaharu Tezuka, Yui Tezuka.
Producer: Etsuko Sato.
Creative Boutique: SAMURAI.
A&P: Jakuetsu.

FUJI KINDERGARTEN

Japanese graphic designer and creative director Kashiwa Sato established the «Samurail» creative studio in 2000. His major works include TV commercial films, art works for musicians, product designs and the creation of visual identities. His ever-expanding visions and creative works in various fields are highly acclaimed and encompass the building and branding of Fuji Kindergarten which is a new kind of kindergarten in Tachikawa, a suburb of Tokyo. Designed in collaboration with architects Takaharu and Yui Tezuka, Fuji Kindergarten's most captivating elements are its circular orientation and the fact that there are no walls (i.e. barriers) at all. Fuji is an open-minded institution known for Montessori teaching methods and aims at providing children with a learning environment that is as holistic as possible.

Joël Tettamanti 2005, *Untitled images from the Studies Lager.*

↗ This former transformer station from the fifties has been converted into a museum for children. Although its limited area of 1,85 x 1,85 metres only allows for use by small people, the museum offers many things to be discovered.

Nalbach + Nalbach Gesellschaft von Architekten mbH 2007, *Kinderhotel des Seehotel am Neuklostersee* Design / J. and G. Nalbach.

OLIFANT

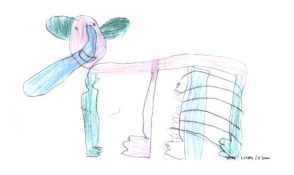

98 / 99

Pictures — ./studio3 - **Institute for Experimental Architecture** 2006, *Olifantsvlei* ^{Design} / Prof. Volker Giencke, DI Astrid Dahmen + 30 students ^{Photography} / Institute for Experimental Architecture ./studio3.

Drawings — ./studio3 - **Children of KIGA Polling** 2006, *Olifantsvlei drawings* ^{Design} / Linn, Rene, Matthias .

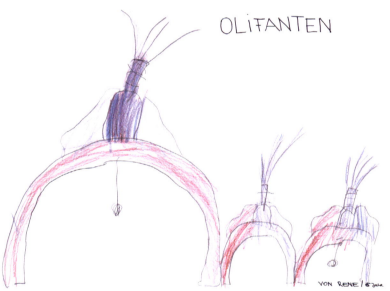

OLIFANTEN

VON RENE / 6 Jahre

FLUG NACH AFRIKA

VON MATTHIAS / 52.

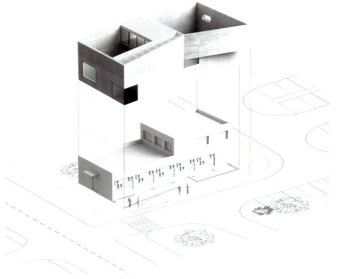

LAN Architecture 2008, *Children's Toy Library - The shell surrounds the core* Design / LAN Architecture Photography / Jean-Marie Monthiers, Paris Description / The visitor experiences the space as soon as he enters the building and crosses the entrance hall, lightened from the façade but also with zenithal glazing taking him to the loan desk. Interior spaces are simply designed, orienting oneself is natural, since serving and served spaces are clearly determined on the two levels.

cercadelcielo Estudio 2007, *ESC Infantil*   Design / cercadelcielo / Joaquin Contreras architect
Photography / David Frutos   Description / contemporary Kindergarten architecture.

Jeremy Bierer 2006, *sans titre*   ^{Photography} / Jeremy Bierer
^{Description} / Illustration contest for the childhood conference,
Geneva, Switzerland, Fall 2006.

70°N Arkitektur 2006, *Kindergartens* , Tromsø ^{Photography} / <u>Ivan Brodey</u>.

↗ The kindergarten is built to guarantee the possibility of variety in the use of rooms. One can change each room into new rooms of various sizes and functions with veryy simple moves. There are several options for combinations and joint actions of rooms and spaces. Flexibility is also guaranteed by the inner walls in every base station (fixed on one end and wheels on the other). They can be rotated like indicators around an axis and be put in different positions making various smaller rooms in the big base room. Furniture and toys are partly integrated in the wall system so that the floor area can be as free as possible: long drawing tables, climbing walls and puppet theatre are all parts of the playing walls.

DIE BAUPILOTEN

Imagine an elementary school transformed into a dragon's lair. Light funnels up from apertures set low in the walls and down from incisions made just below the ceiling. Seating and desktops fold down from the walls like opening petals. As he ascends from the ground to the third floor, the dragon's sylvan, aluminium skeleton is armoured in a shimmering, fireproof, glass-fibre textile, his tail and wings scaled with reflective stainless steel plates. In a stairwell, children create music and learn about harmony by plucking harp strings, tuned in octaves, which are strung along the walls. Imagine a schoolroom that resembles a vast sanctuary made of flowers which, depending on the seasonal position of the sun, use their reflective steel «blossoms» to draw sunlight deep into

- 2 -

- 1 -

1. — **die Baupiloten** 2005, *Kindergarten Tree of Dreams*, ᴰᵉˢⁱᵍⁿ / die Baupiloten
ᴾʰᵒᵗᵒᵍʳᵃᵖʰʸ / Jan Bitter   ᴰᵉˢᶜʳⁱᵖᵗⁱᵒⁿ / Second floor, 'The Throne on the Beat of the Wings', landscape of learning.

2. — 2005, *Kindergarten Tree of Dreams*, ᴰᵉˢⁱᵍⁿ / die Baupiloten
ᴾʰᵒᵗᵒᵍʳᵃᵖʰʸ / Jan Bitter   ᴰᵉˢᶜʳⁱᵖᵗⁱᵒⁿ / Atrium, reflective steel 'leaves'.

the building. At the door, children are greeted in the 14 languages that correspond to the neighbourhoods' ethnic make-up.

In Berlin's Wedding district, where the dragon-infested Erika Mann Elementary School is located, half of the students' parents are unemployed and 85% hail from immigrant families. Since the renovation of the school, however, surveys have demonstrated that two-thirds of Mann graduates go on to attend an intermediate or high school and comparative tests of its fourth graders test 20% higher than the city average.

'I don't have children but I enjoy working with them immensely,' admits Susanne Hofmann, founder of the architecture practice, die Baupiloten, which has metamorphosed a few of Berlin's kindergartens and elementary schools – according to their students' wishes. 'We inspire each other: They delve into a world we suggest and we entertain their ideas and fantastic imaginary world. Together we wonder where their collages might lead, we discuss their ideas of merry-go-rounds made of flowers or the fact that the school should fly.'

Hofmann established die Baupiloten as part of the Technical University of Berlin with 11 university architecture students in order to renovate the drably severe 1915 Mann school building that Hofmann describes as 'a typical product of spartan Prussian architecture that exudes a daunting authority.' During the first stage of the project, her students brought enough materials for a group of 20 third to sixth graders to make paper collages describing a 'path through the garden of the future.' In response, the children invented fictional lands with

such titles as «The Hot Garden» and «The Garden of Traces». 'Listening to the pupils describing their imaginary landscapes with a very explicit and sensuous vocabulary was inspiring,' Hofmann says. 'In their thoughts they led us through an airy, golden, icy, soft, cushioned, fluffy, feathery, furry, cuddly, tight, bright, dreary, wispy, stretchy, prickly world.'

Of course, as every schoolchild knows and most architects have been taught to forget, form follows fiction. From descriptions as expressive as these and from observations of the children at work and play, die Baupiloten created (as it does for most of its school projects) collages, photomontages, models and life-size, interactive prototypes to communicate their architectural ideas to the school's faculty and the children every few weeks, in order to elicit their – unexpectedly articulate – feedback. In this manner, the kids – or should we say the clients – helped to design their own environments. 'The pupils longed for an architecture that glows, resonates, alters and somehow «lives»,' recalls Hofmann. 'Their desires were taken seriously and their decisions respected. The school became their place of identity and support in a difficult district. It became a place they could relate to. It became their school.'

5. — 2003, *Erika Mann Elementary School I,* ^{Design} / die Baupiloten
^{Photography} / Jan Bitter ^{Description} / First floor, 'Breath of Gentle Air'.

- 5 -

- 3 -

3. — **die Baupiloten** 2005, *Kindergarten Tree of Dreams* ^{Design} / die Baupiloten ^{Photography} / Jan Bitter ^{Description} / Ground floor, evening glow.

4. — **die Baupiloten** 2005, *Kindergarten Tree of Dreams* ^{Design} / die Baupiloten ^{Photography} / Jan Bitter ^{Description} / Ground floor, winter a-sparkle.

- 4 -

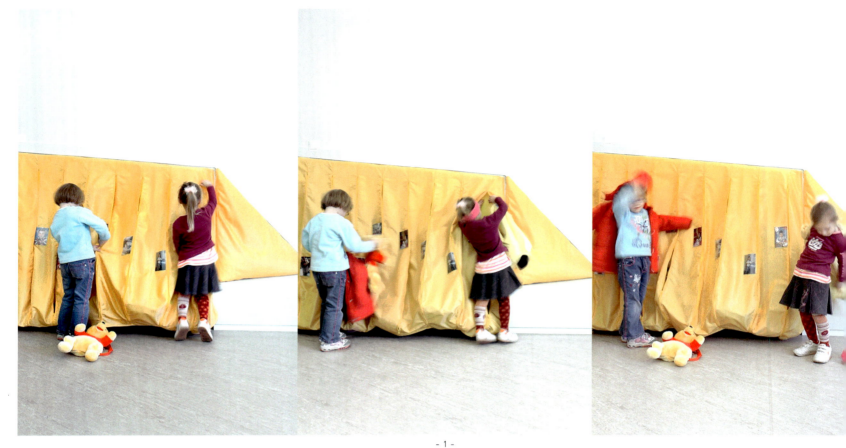

- 1 -

- 2 -

108 / 109

- 3 -

1. — **die Baupiloten** 2007, *Kindergarten Taka-Tuka-Land* ^{Design} / die Baupiloten ^{Photography} / Jan Bitter ^{Description} / Lemonade Wardrobe-Drops.

2. — 2003, *Erika Mann Elementary School I* ^{Design} / die Baupiloten ^{Photography} / Jan Bitter ^{Description} / Third floor.

3. — 2003, *Erika Mann Elementary School I* ^{Design} / die Baupiloten ^{Photography} / Jan Bitter ^{Description} / Ground floor.

4. — 2005, *Kindergarten Tree of Dreams* ^{Design} / die Baupiloten ^{Photography} / Jan Bitter ^{Description} / Ground floor.

5. — 2005, *Kindergarten Tree of Dreams* ^{Design} / die Baupiloten ^{Photography} / Jan Bitter ^{Description} / First floor.

- 1 -

- 2 -

110 / 111

1. — **die Baupiloten** 2007, *Kindergarten Taka-Tuka-Land* ^{Design} / die Baupiloten ^{Photography} / Jan Bitter ^{Description} / Eastern façade, climbing bark.

2. — 2007, *Kindergarten Taka-Tuka-Land*, ^{Design} / die Baupiloten ^{Photography} / Jan Bitter ^{Description} / Secret passage way.

3. — 2007, *Kindergarten Taka-Tuka-Land* ^{Design} / die Baupiloten ^{Photography} / Jan Bitter ^{Description} / Southern façade, spotting friends.

4. — 2007, *Kindergarten Taka-Tuka-Land* ^{Design} / die Baupiloten ^{Photography} / Jan Bitter ^{Description} / Delving into the lemonade.

HOME SWEET HOME

....

When considering the decoration of homes, take a look at the new generation of
colourful and interchangeable sets of wall stickers by designers Marielle Baldelli and Sébastien Messerschmidt of Lyon-based E-Glue, a studio specialising in
concept and design for kids: "Characters from our childhood are obviously the
starting point of our work but the goal is now to add our graphic and design research, which means creating our own identity,' says Messerschmidt. 'We realise
that childhood imagery is pre-conditioned and that many parents don't dare to not
uphold these «clichés».

   When it comes to private space, clichés are close at hand because a
   home does not merely have just one function, but serves a series of different needs to be fulfilled as different kinds of people and genera-
   tions live together, thus having to share their daily routines. What is
   home? Home is where the family gathers socially, like in the kitchen or
   in the living room. Home is where space is shared, but used individu-
   ally, as with, for instance, the toilet. And last but not least, home is
   where everyone needs to have their very own retreat, which is why children love to build their own world within the one that already exists -
   think of the cozy cave that almost every kid has created with whatever
   was at hand.

Hence, home's interior design is not an easy one to agree upon. On the one hand
a parent's idea of style is often too sophisticated for children. On the other
hand a child's free-spirited ideas of a well-designed home might clash with the
ones of their procreators. At the latest when the latter finds walls painted with
mud or when the bedroom is decked out in fluorescent yellow… Not to mention the
hard-to-exterminate omnipresence of teddy bear motifs on far too many children's
products (wallpaper, pillows, cups). Admittedly, this is no great help when it
comes to coordinating the décor in the nursery with that of the living room.

   HOME SWEET HOME presents tasteful items for use in the home. Items and
   furniture that are as sustainable as they are well-designed, but nei-
   ther too expensive nor too stylish. There is colourful furniture that is
   made of better material than most of last century's throwaway culture
   has ever provided for, and which offers a different type of functionality and inspiration for kids to play with and bring into play. The examples in this chapter show how creativity and necessity can be in sync,
   providing homes that are as comfortable as they are acceptable for both
   children and adults. This special selection of multi-functional and inspiring items, objects and furniture mirrors the multi-faceted reality we live in and presents new ideas and playful ways of furnishing in
   what is undoubtedly the most important place for children in the whole
   wide world: Home.

....

3

- 1 -

1. — **LULA** 2008, *Buclo & Hus* ^{Design} / <u>Ulrika Engberg</u> ^{Photography} / <u>Elisabeth</u> <u>Dunker</u> ^{Manufacturer} / <u>Little Red Stuga</u> ^{Description} / Styling and photography for the Swedish kids' brand, Little Red Stuga.

2. — 2008, *Hus* ^{Design} / <u>Little Red Stuga design studio</u> ^{Photography} / <u>Elisabeth Dunker</u> ^{Manufacturer} / <u>Little Red Stuga</u> ^{Description} / Hus is a play screen that also works as a room divider. It was developed together with children in a kindergarten.

- 2 -

3 + 4 . — 2007, *Dream Bag* ^{Design} / <u>Little Red Stuga design studio</u> ^{Photography} / <u>Elisabeth Dunker</u> ^{Manufacturer} / <u>Little Red Stuga</u> ^{Description} / Dream Bag is a comfy floor cushion for small children to rest on, play with or to dream away in. Size 100 cm, limited edition.

5. — 2008, *Kebnekaise knitted pouf* ^{Design} / <u>Little Red Stuga Design studio</u> ^{Photography} / <u>Little Red Stuga</u> ^{Manufacturer} / <u>Little Red Stuga</u> ^{Material} / Upholstered in cotton and filled with polystyrene balls ^{Description} / Kebnekaise is the highest mountain in Sweden at 2104 m and is situated in the north of Sweden. Now every child can climb it in the living room. Made in Sweden. Diameter 60 cm.

Anna Blattert 2006, *Jäkälä domestic landscape* ^{Design} / <u>An-na Blattert, Claudia Heiniger</u> ^{Photography} / <u>Bernhard Gardell.</u>

↗ Jäkälä allows the creativity of both children and adults to roam freely. Jäkälä can be used in many different ways. The reclosable fasteners allow experimentation with two-dimensional paths and patterns, as well as with rises, bulges, and towers. The result is a domestic landscape. The rubber-coated rear side protects it from moisture, and makes Jäkälä also usable outdoors. This variability of use and the many ways in which the forms can be combined supports collective designing.

bObles 2005, *Tumbling Animals* Photography / Christian Alsing
Material / Firm foam – non-toxin.

Top — **Kristian Kutschera** 2008, *New York subway-blackboard for future graffiti-writers* ^{Design} / Kristian Kutschera ^{Photographer} / bürokutschera ^{Material} / Blackboard-paint and silver spray-paint on MDF ^{Description} / Blackboard in the shape of a Bronx-bound New York subway car.

Bottom — **Yael Mer & Shay Alkalay | Raw-Edges** 2008, *Plastic Nostalgia* ^{Design} / Yael Mer & Shay Alkalay ^{Manufacturer} / Arts Co ^{Material} / Ready-made Fisher-Price toy parts from the 70s in wood.

Top — **studiomama** 2002, *Kids House* ^{Design} / studiomama - Nina Tolstrup ^{Photography} / Stine Raarup ^{Manufacturer} / studiomama ^{Material} / Painted MDF, with blackboard on one side and Lego panels on the other. 2 x 2,2 x 1,8 m ^{Description} / The kids house was built as a playful structure that could serve both as a sleeping space or playhouse.

Bottom — 2008, *Kids House made of recycled doors* ^{Design} / studiomama - Nina Tolstrup ^{Material} / Painted MDF, with blackboard on one side and Lego panels on the other. 2 x 2,2 x 1,8 m ^{Description} / Recycled doors.

- 1 -

- 2 -

1. — **Stud o Maartje Steenkamp** 2004, *Highchair* ^{Design} / Maartje Steenkamp ^{Photography} / Inga Powilleit
^{Manufacturer} / Production by SMS ^{Material} / White beechwood H. 145 cm W. 62 cm D. 59 cm. Sizes in box: H 137 cm B 66 cm D 8,5 cm.

↗ This long-legged child's chair is based on the growth of a child. A small child likes to be carried around and observe the world around him on the same eye level as the parent. The bigger the child gets, the less it needs the help of its parents help. By sawing down the legs, the parent makes a physical statement to help its child get more and more independent. In the same sense it is a mark in time. The chair will never get its long legs back, the same way you cannot turn time; your child will never be small again. The phases of the chair are identical with different steps in the life of the child.

- 3 -

2 + 3 — 2006, *Childchildchair* ^{Design} / Maartje Steenkamp ^{Photography} / Inga Powilleit ^{Manufacturer} / Production by SMS ^{Material} / Birch multiplex H. 63 cm W. 78 cm D. 53 cm ^{Description} / This combination of two children's chairs and a small table is a playful variation on the idea of the Mother Child Dining.

- 4 -

- 5 -

- 6 -

4. — **Studio Maartje Steenkamp** 2002, *Rubchair* ^{Design} / Maartje Steenkamp ^{Photography} / Inga Powilleit ^{Manufacturer} / Prototype ^{Material} / Soft polyurethane, wood H. 68 cm high position H. 54 cm W. 34 cm D. 34 cm ^{Description} / This chair is based on the archetype chair. You can turn the small chair into a real chair by simply turning the legs.

5 + 6 — **De la Espada** 2008, *035 Tone Kids Table* ^{Design} / Leif.design-park ^{Manufacturer} / Atlantico ^{Material} / Solid American black walnut ^{Description} / Tone Kids Table, made from solid planks of American black walnut, has an understated modern form that makes it a fitting accompaniment to the delectable parquetry of the Tone Kids Chair.

7 - 9. — **Paul Blease** 2008, *Treasure chest of drawers* ^{Material} / Walnut with brushed steel handles ^{Manufacturer} / Beingblease. com ^{Description} / A project that focuses on the emotional economy of family and the revision of family rituals through playful modular furniture. Treasure chest captures the imagination of children whilst providing a suitable amount of storage for adults. Drawers pull out in every direction revealing hidden treasures and surprises.

- 7 -

- 8 -

- 9 -

- 1 -

- 2 -

1 + 2 — **KOON Co.** 2005, *Pony Table Set*   Design / Aracho   Manufacturer / KOON   Material / Wooden frame covered with stress-resistant polyurethane foam in fabric upholstery   Description / A multi-purpose table set for children that must be suitable in various public or commercial areas. Pony itself can be turned and placed just as the child wishes or can be inserted in the table like a jigsaw puzzle. When chairs are placed together they form a sofa.

3. — **Floris Hovers** 2008, *Read Mobile*   Design / Floris Hovers   Material / Birch plywood   Description / Mobile book cupboard with reading desk and seat.

4. — 2008, *Chair to read*   Designer / Floris Hovers   Material / Pine   Description / Chair to read for parents.

- 3 -

- 4 -

- 5 -

- 6 -

- 7 -

5. — **Judith Drews** 2008, *DOT Chair*   Design / Judith Drews
Photography / Hans Baltzer   Manufacturer / Atelier Flora   Material / Wood   Description / Chair for children.

6 + 7. — **Yael Mer & Shay Alkalay | Raw-Edges** 2006, *Rocking Slippers*   Design / Yael Mer
Manufacturer / Self production.

8. — **Balouga** 2007, *Kazam 01*   Design / Mahmoud Akram   Photography / Marie Pierre Morel
Manufacturer / Balouga Edition   Material / Moulded plywood, laminate, steel   Description / Evolutionary desk. Buy one desk, get three sizes for infant to adult.

- 8 -

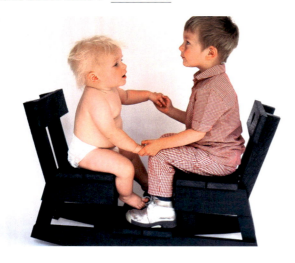

INEKE HANS

In the summer of 2001, Dutch designer Ineke Hans established a children's collection called Black Beauties: Thirteen products with some very traditional small items for boys (crash car) and girls (skipping rope).

She says that this project had already been unknowingly started earlier: "The first Black Beauty was «Wet Step», which was made in 2000 for friends who had gotten married and were rebuilding their bathroom. For the birthday of another friend, who collected children's chairs, «Office Chair» was made, while «Up/down Chair» was made on request. All items are made of black recycled plastic: Wind-, water-, salt-, acid- and UV-resistant." The material allows products like the bathroom step and the swings to be put outdoors and used in wet environments. "The decision to make them in the black material came when designing colourful work years before, and observing that most materials are available in white, natural and black. More importantly, the Black Beauties show that children do not only react to colours, but very often respond to shapes, opportunities and ways of playing with things."

In some ways the project is closely connected to earlier projects of Ineke Hans, like «Seven Chairs in Seven Days» and «Under Cover Chairs», their designs being associative, clear and playing with functions.

Clockwise from top — **Ineke Hans** 2001, *Share Chairs, Crash Car, Sing Swing, Office Desk, Springtime* Design / <u>Ineke Hans</u>
Material / Recycled plastic   Manufacturer / <u>Inekehans©ollection</u>.

Clockwise from left — 2001, *Double Trouble*, *Up-Down Chair*,
Supperman, Rock Stock, Happy Horse Design / Ineke Hans
Material / Recycled plastic Manufacturer / Inekehans©ollection.

1. — **Balouga** 2007, *Kazam 02* ^{Design} / Mahmoud Akram
^{Photography} / Marie Pierre ^{Manufactura} / Balouga Edition
^{Material} / Moulded plywood, laminate, steel ^{Description} / Evolutionary desk with a comfortable working surface.

2. — **De La Espada** 2009, *Fura Kids Rocker* ^{Design} / Leif.designpark ^{Material} / Powder-coated steel ^{Manufacturer} / Atlantico ^{Description} / A modern interpretation of the classic rocking horse. A contour of painted steel provides the framework for a dancing sensation.

3. — 2009, *Lotta Kids Sofa* ^{Design} / Leif.designpark ^{Material} / Powder-coated steel and wool or cotton upholstery ^{Manufacturer} / Atlantico ^{Description} / Lotta allows children to sit together, talking, laughing and playing on a modern form that will be the envy of their parents.

4. — 2009, *Ketta Kids Chair* ^{Design} / Leif.designpark ^{Material} / American black walnut or American white oak ^{Manufacturer} / Atlantico ^{Description} / This kids' chair has storage space behind the backrest for storing books, or any of the child's favourite objects, making the chair the child's base.

- 1 -

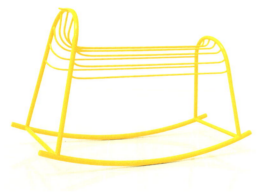

- 2 -

- 3 -

- 4 -

5.— **PearsonLloyd Design Ltd.** 2008, *Rocky* Design / PearsonLloyd Manufacturer / MO by Martinez Otero Photography / © nuriacarballo Material / Laminated wood.

6. — **Kloss** 2007, *Ponny* Design / Ole Petter Wullum Manufacturer / Kloss Photographer / Kloss Material / Plywood.

7. — 2007, *Giraffe* Design / Ole Petter Wullum Manufacturer / Kloss Photographer / Kloss Material / Plywood.

8. — 2007, *Tassen* Design / Ole Petter Wullum Manufacturer / Kloss Photographer / Kloss Material / Plywood.

- 5 -

- 6 -

- 7 -

- 8 -

- 1 -

1. — **Martino Gamper** 2003, *The Get Together Sofa 05* ^{Design} / Martino Gamper ^{Material} / Leather, cardboard tube, foam, buttons, mirror, fabric, ratchet straps.

↗ This project adresses the psycho-social aspects of furniture design. Beyond their geometric definitions, corners are either places to feel safe and at peace, to dwell on private thoughts but can also be claus-trophobic or isolating. By pushing back toward the room's edges, Martino seeks out social interaction that is less polite, but more compelling.

2. — **KOON Co.** 2008, *Apple Tree* ^{Design} / Hye Young Park
^{Material} / Black board on MDF, a chair and prop in birch plywood.

- 2 -

– 3 –

– 4 –

– 5 –

3. — **Atelier Charivari** 2008, *Atelier Charivari vintage school desk.*

4. — 2008, *vintage cradle*   Material / Wood, inox.

5. —2008, *vintage 50's bed*   Material / Wood, inox.

6. — **KOON Co.** 2008, *Just Sit (wherever you sit is the chair)*
Design / Young Woo Kim & Seung Heum Park   Material / Birch plywood with fabric upholstery   Description / A drawing on the surface of the box names the box for a stool to 'sit on'. A real model of the stool is also created in the same scale as the drawing
on the box. The box itself can be either a package for the stool
or used as storage for other objects.

7. — 2008, *Rooney's Bench*   Design / Ji Yoon Jeong & Young Hee
Lee   Manufacturer / KOON, Little KooN   Material / Birch plywood with
fabric upholstery, MDF.

– 6 –

– 7 –

1. — **Katrin Olina Petursdottir** 2005, *Junior Tree* Design / Katrin Olina Photography / swedese Manufacturer / swedese Material / Plywood and lacquered wood.

2. — **cardboardesign** 2008, *The Lemonade Advice Stand and Palm tree* Photography / Cathy Henszey Material / Recycled cardboard.

3. — 2008, *Doggie Stool* Design / Ben Blanc Material / Recycled corrugated cardboard Description / Stools of all different kinds of animals.

4. — **KOON Co.** 2004, *Totibox* Design / Aracho Photography / KOON Manufacturer / KOON Material / Birch plywood with fabric upholstery.

- 1 -

- 2 -

- 3 -

- 4 -

130 / 131

- 5 -

- 6 -

5 - 6. — **Villa Carton** 2007, *Cardboard Rocking Chair*
Design / <u>Villa Carton</u> Manufacturer / <u>Villa Carton</u> Material / Cardboard.

7. — **Corraini Edizioni** 1967/2008, *Wall* Design / <u>Enzo Mari</u>
Manufacturer / <u>Corraini Edizioni</u> Material / Corrugated pressboard.

Life Time Furniture 2007, *Treehouse*   Photography / Ede Lukkien   Manufacturer / M. Schack Engel A/S, Denmark   Material / High quality European pine grown in ecological forestry; coloured MDF fronts.

↗ The Life Time treehouse is the tough version of the mini canopy bed. The modular structure allows for easy accessibility while the imaginative half-open design means that there is always light and space in the treehouse. Once the occupant feels things are getting too cramped, it's easy to convert the bed back into a standard mini bunk bed or basic bed.

Top — **KOON Co.** 2008, *Toti-bunk* ^{Design} / Aracho
^{Photography} / KOON ^{Manufacturer} / KOON, Little KooN ^{Material} / Birch
plywood with fabrics upholstery, MDF frame veneered with
fine natural wood disk - plywood with a lacquered metal
structure ^{Description} / A total package of bunk bed series that
merges all the playful and functional utilities with multi-
level arrangements where sleep, play and study are united.
Additional parts and units really maximise space utilisa-
tion of a kid's room.

Bottom — 2005, *Totiblock* ^{Design} / Aracho
^{Photography} / KOON ^{Manufacturer} / KOON, Little KooN ^{Material} / Birch
plywood with fabric upholstery MDF frame veneered with
fine natural wood ^{Description} / A bookcase for kids which
combines play and function, used as either storage or decoration. Add-on the doors in birch plywood with upholstery
and make use of the space for memory games or storage.

1. — **Kloss** 2007, *Kloss Shelves* Design / Ole Petter Wullum
Manufacturer / Kloss Material / Plywood.

2. — 2007, *Kloss Bench & Kloss Table* Design / Ole Petter
Wullum Manufacturer / Kloss Material / Plywood.

3 + 4. — 2007, *Puzzle Petit* Design / Ole Petter Wullum
Manufacturer / Kloss Material / Plywood, solid birch.

- 1 -

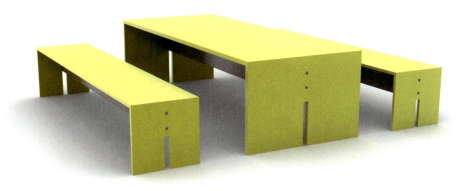

- 2 -

- 3 -

- 4 -

- 1 -

- 2 -

1. — **Company** 2007, *Mushroom Stool* ^{Design} / <u>Company (Aamu Song & Johan Olin)</u> ^{Photography} / <u>Lee Inhee</u> ^{Manufacturer} / <u>Company</u> ^{Material} / Birch.

2. — Machabang5 ^{Photography} / <u>Lee Inhee</u>.

3. — 2008, *Dog Stools* ^{Design} / <u>Company (Aamu Song & Johan Olin)</u> ^{Photography} / <u>Lee Inhee</u> ^{Manufacturer} / <u>Company</u>.

- 3 -

4. — **Balouga** 2008, *Miles Rug*   Design / Big Game
Photography / Julie Ansiau   Manufacturer / Balouga Edition
Material / Wool   Description / Hand tufted woven carpet. Colour of
the client's choice.

5. — 2008, *Kalo System*   Design / Mahmoud Akram
Photography / Mahmoud Akram   Manufacturer / Balouga Edition
Material / Moulded plywood, laminate   Description / Wall mount-
able shelving system. Easy to assemble. For books, files,
small object and toys.

6. — **Itay Ohaly** 2008, *Papa chair*   Design / Itay Ohaly
Photography / Itay Ohaly   Material / Wood   Description / The 'Papa chair'
is a family of chairs and aims at encouraging the interaction between parent and child.

- 4 -

- 5 -

- 6 -

Morgen 2008, *Morgen Kids* Design / Sabine Mühlbauer Manufacturer / Morgen Studio Photography / Thorsten Ruppert Material / 12 mm strong phenol coated multiplex plate Description / This adjustable collection by MORGEN is designed to "grow up" with your kids and is a combination of shape, function and design. The children's bed also turns into a couch and the changing table converts into a chest of drawers with a CD rack.

Ab Rogers 2004, *Kenny Schachter* ᴰᵉˢⁱᵍⁿ / Ab Rogers Design with Shona Kitchen ᴾʰᵒᵗᵒᵍʳᵃᵖʰʸ / Morley van Sternberg ᴰᵉˢᶜʳⁱᵖᵗⁱᵒⁿ / A large double fronted Victorian house in Chelsea is the residency of art dealer, Kenny Schachter, his fashion designer wife and their four children under 10. They commissioned ARD, in partnership with Shona Kitchen, to create a series of interventions throughout their house.

In the children's area on the second and third floor a unique playroom and kids' bedroom exists. It is as if 4 pods from another planet have landed in this Victorian house. The pods contain desks, PlayStations, TVs and integrated mattresses. The colours and specific designs are based on the children's personal fantasies and imagination. An exhilarating slide connects the third floor to the second.

- 1 -

1. — **Our Children's Gorilla** 2003, *Children Unite*
Design / <u>Hampus Ericstam</u>   Manufacturer / <u>Our Children's Gorilla</u>   Material / Swan eco labled recycled paper   Description / A poster inspired by the graphics of African 60's propaganda era.

2. — 2003, *Twins*   Design / <u>Our Children's Gorilla</u>   Manufacturer / <u>Our Children's Gorilla</u>   Material / Recyclable semi-transparent paper   Description / A mobile.

3. — 2007, *Lucha Catman*   Design / <u>Our Children's Gorilla</u>   Manufacturer / <u>Our Children's Gorilla</u>   Material / E1 certified MDF, waterbased laquer   Description / A jigsaw puzzle inspired by Mexican wrestling masks.

- 2 -

- 3 -

Clockwise from top — **Kideko** 2007, *Love and Sunshine, Action and Beauty, Action and Monster Poster* Design / Kirsty Bruce Photography / Tim Robinson Manufacturer / Kideko Material / Screen print on paper Description / Large hand-made silk screen printed posters.

- 1 -

- 2 -

ATELIER XT

'Our inspiration is found by living a simple life in which the handmade is greatly appreciated,' says Graça Paz who, with her husband Francisco Pereira da Costa, makes up the Porto, Portugal-based design studio, Atelier XT. 'We believe that a piece of furniture can grow with a kid into its adult life and even be passed on to his or her children.'

XT's hand-crafted and hand-painted furniture, objects and interiors are wrought with colour and evoke effortless solidity. In its sturdiness, simplicity and often nature-oriented décor, every piece of furniture communicates a connection to the firmament and solid ground alike. The couple wanted to create something antithetical in a market crowded with industrial products and dominated by waste. Paz believes that today's furniture is treated like a small accessory, easily thrown away only to be replaced with an even more easily disposable version.

The designers have four boys for whom they have always made furniture, but they finally began to design for kids commercially after searching for existing products only to discover, explains Paz, 'that the market needed something really different. Our blue cradle, Antonio, was made for Antonio, our youngest son, after look-

- 3 -

1. — **Atelier XT** 2007, *untitled* Design / Graça Paz Manufacturer / Atelier XT
Material / Wood, paper Description / 3D painting.

2. — 2007, *Baby Blanket* Design / Graça Paz Manufacturer / Atelier XT
Material / 100% wool Description / Handmade and unique piece.

3. — 2008, *Shop window by Atelier XT* Design / Francisco Pereira da Costa,
Graça Paz Manufacturer / Atelier XT Material / Wood, fabric, paper
Description / Project for a shop window.

- 4 -

- 5 -

- 6 -

- 7 -

ing for cradles in the stores. My kids are my inspiration – and they are our way of testing our work.'

Da Costa has an architecture degree but also designs and builds furniture that reflects his approach to both life and architecture: Strong, robust and safe, eschewing anything superfluous. His perfect complement, Paz, who studied fashion design but has always worked with interiors and urban crafts, and as a painter, adds elements that some modern designers would call wholly superfluous: Character and colour.

'We believe in colour and its connection to feelings and reason in everyday life,' Paz says. 'Children must learn colour in relation to objects and must be told to look and see at the same time, to «capture».' When Francisco passes a piece he has constructed on to Paz for finishing, she makes each unique; partly because, not being a machine, it is difficult for her to hand-paint everything identically, but mostly because she prefers it that way. Paz revels in mixing patterns ('I'm not afraid to use and abuse patterns and colour!') and creating characters that imbue an object with feeling and bring it, dare we say, to life.

4. — 2007, *Antonio cradle* Design / Francisco Pereira da Costa, Graça Paz Manufacturer / Atelier XT Material / Solid German pine wood Description / Baby cradle that is easy for children to climb out of in the morning.

5. — 2007, *Birds sculpture* Design / Graça Paz Manufacturer / Atelier XT Material / Fabric Description / 'Good luck' small sculpture bird.

6. — 2008, *Francisco cradle* Design / Francisco Pereira da Costa, Graça Paz Manufacturer / Atelier XT Material / Solid German pine wood Description / Baby cradle for safe sleep and play.

7. — 2006, *Julieta sculpture doll* Design / Graça Paz Manufacturer / Atelier XT Material / Fabric Description / Sculptured play doll.

Home Sweet Home / Atelier XT

1. — **Atelier XT** 2007, *Shelves on wheels* ^{Design} / Francisco Pereira da Costa, Graça Paz ^{Manufacturer} / Atelier XT ^{Material} / Solid German pine wood ^{Description} / A mobile shelf for books and toys.

2. — 2004, *Antonio newborn crib* ^{Design} / Francisco Pereira da Costa, Graça Paz ^{Manufacturer} / Atelier XT ^{Material} / Solid German pine wood ^{Description} / Crib with wooden weels and a shelf for books and toys.

3. — 2007, *Baby Room Composition* ^{Design} / Francisco Pereira da Costa, Graça Paz ^{Manufacturer} / Atelier XT ^{Description} / Baby room composition in a Portuguese interiors fair.

4. — 2006, *Chest of drawers* ^{Design} / Francisco Pereira da Costa, Graça Paz ^{Manufacturer} / Atelier XT ^{Material} / Solid German pine wood ^{Description} / Handmade chest of drawers with an unique flowers pattern.

- 1 -

- 2 -

- 3 -

- 4 -

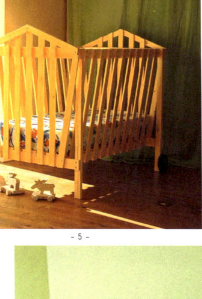

5 + 8. — 2004, *Carolina cradle* Design / Francisco Pereira da Costa and Graça Paz Manufacturer / Atelier XT Material / Solid German plain wood Description / Cradle for save sleep and play.

6 + 7. — 2005, *Twins working table* Design / Francisco Pereira da Costa and Graça Paz Manufacturer / Atelier XT Material / Solid German plain wood Description / This car doubles as a work table with a storage box below.

↗ The Twins Table was a special order from a client who gave birth to twins.

- 1 -

- 2 -

- 3 -

- 4 -

1. — **Miko Design** 2006, *Bedroom of Sofia and Mila*
Design / Erika Harberts, Radovan Milosevic Photographer / <u>Erika Harberts</u> Manufacturer / <u>Homemade</u> Material / MDF
Description / Two girls share a small bedroom so the beds are raised for more storage area and made into two little houses for imaginative play.

2. — 2006, *Bedroom of Sofia and Mila* Design / <u>Mikodesign</u> Photographer / <u>Erika Harberts</u> Manufacturer / <u>Mikodesign</u>
Material / Cotton, felt Description / A curtain to make a little girls bed into a little flower house.

3. — 2007, *Desk* Design / Mikodesign Photographer / <u>Erika Harberts</u> Manufacturer / <u>Homemade</u> Material / MDF Description / Two little desks and some rope create a little space for a small artist.

4. — 2007, *Mila in the play kitchen* Design / <u>Erika Harberts</u> Photographer / <u>Erika Harberts</u> Manufacturer / <u>Homemade</u>
Material / Old CD cabinet with some old shelves Description / This little play area with recycled materials was made in just one day.

- 5 -

- 6 -

- 7 -

- 8 -

5. — **Judith Zaugg** 2005, *Ufo* Design / Judith Zaugg (Illustration)
Photography / Rolf Siegenthaler Material / Print on a small plexiglass lightbox.

6. — 2005, *Abseits* Design / Judith Zaugg (Illustration)
Photography / Rolf Siegenthaler Material / Print on an old medicine lightbox.

7. — 2005, *Ufo* Design / Judith Zaugg (Illustration)
Photography / Rolf Siegenthaler wMaterial / Print on a small plexiglass lightbox.

8 — 2005, *Lemon-Man* Design / Judith Zaugg (Illustration)
Photography / Rolf Siegenthaler Material / Print on an old train station lightbox.

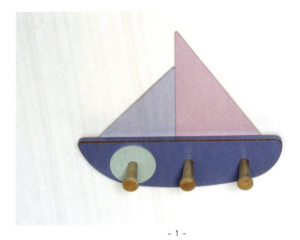

- 1 -

- 2 -

- 3 -

1. — **Pastel Toys** 2003, *Boat Triple Hanger* Manufacturer / PastelToys
Material / Wood, MDF.

2 + 3. — **Judith Zaugg** 2005, *Flieger*, Tisch & Stuhl Design / Judith Zaugg
(Illustration) Photography / Rolf Siegenthaler Manufacturer / Collaboration with the
furniture designer Tiger Romig Material / Print on HPL (high-pressure-lami-
nate) and wood.

4. — **Lorena Siminovich** 2008, *Petit Collage Animal Alphabet* Design / Lorena
Siminovich Photography / Annie Tsou Manufacturer / Petit Collage Material / Water
based inks, 100% post-consumer recycled paper.

5. — 2006, *Elephant Splash* Design / Lorena Siminovich Photography / Annie
Tsou Manufacturer / Petit Collage Material / Vintage, found and painted papers on
FSC certified maple plywood.

- 4 -

- 5 -

- 6 -

6. — **Hikje Janneke Zantinge** 2008, Animal wallsoftie
Design / Janneke Zantinge Manufacturer / Hikje
Material / Felt, cotton.

7. — 2008, *Elephant&co wallsoftie* Design / Janneke
Zantinge Manufacturer / Hikje Material / Felt, cotton
Comment / The little radio and factory-lamp are also
made by Janneke Zantinge.

8. — 2008, *Wallsoftie fish, crane and elephant*
Design / Janneke Zantinge Manufacturer / Hikje Material / Felt,
cotton.

9. — **Lorena Siminovich** 2007, *Blue Owl Family Collage*
Design / Lorena Siminovich Photography / Annie Tsou
Manufacturer / Petit Collage Material / Vintage, painted, and
found papers on FSC certified maple plywood.

- 7 -

- 9 -

- 8 -

- 1 -

1. — **WallCandy Arts** 2008, *RoCoco* ^{Material} / <u>WallCandy</u>
^{Material} / Removable non-toxic wall art / decoration.

2. — 2008, *ChalkBoard Tree* ^{Design} / <u>WallCandy</u>
^{Material} / Removable non-toxic wall art / decoration.

3. — 2008, *ChalkBoard Animals* ^{Design} / <u>Rad Racers</u>
^{Material} / Removable non-toxic wall art / decoration.

4. — 2008, *Growing Tree Growth Chart* ^{Design} / <u>WallCandy</u> ^{Material} / Removable non-toxic wall art / decoration.

- 2 -

- 4 -

- 3 -

Bureau Mario Lombardo 2008, *BML Blackboard*
Design / <u>Bureau Mario Lombardo</u> Photography / <u>Markus Mrugalla</u> Material / MDF board, blackboard.

- 1 -

- 2 -

- 3 -

1. — **Atelier Mijnes** 2008, *Hippo Wallcushion*   Design / Miriam de Boer
Material / 100% wool felt, cotton.

2. — 2007, *Wallhanging Frogs*   Design / Miriam de Boer   Material / 100% wool
felt, frogsound, cotton.

3. — 2007, *Cushion Bird*   Design / Miriam de Boer   Material / 100% wool felt.

4. — **Atelier Mijnes** 2008, *Wallhanging Sea* ^{Design} / <u>Miriam de Boer</u> ^{Material} / 100% wool felt, cotton.

5. — 2008, *Musicowl 'who's dreaming'* ^{Design} / <u>Miriam de Boer</u> ^{Material} / 100% wool felt, cotton, music box.

6. — 2008, *Storage box bird* ^{Design} / <u>Miriam de Boer</u> ^{Material} / 100% wool felt, cotton, wood.

7. — 2009, *Musicbox Owl* ^{Design} / <u>Miriam de Boer</u> ^{Material} / 100% wool felt, music box, cotton.

8. — 2007, *Storagebox-bird* ^{Design} / <u>Miriam de Boer</u> ^{Material} / 100% wool felt, cotton, wood.

9. — 2007, *Storagebox-hippo* ^{Design} / <u>Miriam de Boer</u> ^{Material} / 100% wool felt, plastic cars, cotton.

- 5 -   - 6 -   - 7 -

- 8 -   - 9 -

Clockwise from top — **AREAWARE** 2005, *Rabbit pillow, Terrier Mini Pillow, Zebra pillow, Gorilla mini pillow, Wolf pillow* ^{Design} / FAUNA by Ross Menuez ^{Manufacturer} / AREAWARE ^{Material} / Organic cotton canvas, Polyfil, environmentally friendly soy based inks.

- 2 -

1. — **blabla KIDS** 2007, *Jungle Mobile* Design / Florence Wetterwald Manufacturer / blabla Material / Hand knit 100% cotton.

2. — **Judith Drews** 2007, *Cuddly Devil* Design / Judith Drews, Astrid Tiedt Manufacturer / Lilliberlin Material / Cotton, wool.

3. — **Salon Elfi Berlin** 2008, *Pillows with Animals*
Design / Verena Schaetzlein Manufacturer / Salon Elfi
Material / Hand-silkscreen print on cotton.

4. — **Roadside Projects** 2008, *Flight by Kite*
Design / Jayme McGowan Manufacturer / Roadside Projects
Material / Mixed media on panel.

- 1 -

- 3 -

- 4 -

- 1 -

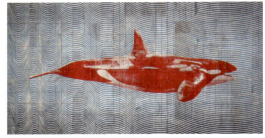

- 2 -

↗ An archival photograph is superimposed on a background created from another photograph creating a multi-layered art piece. The balsa wood tiles on which the image is hand silkscreened adds another layer of texture for visual impact. The inks used on the balsa wall hangings are friendly to the environment (no petroleum). Each piece is signed and numbered by the artist and is available in a limited edition of 300.

- 3 -

1. — **AREAWARE** 2005, *Monster Balsa* ^{Design} / <u>FAUNA by Ross Menuez</u> ^{Manufacturer} / <u>AREAWARE</u> ^{Material} / Balsa wood, cotton canvas, environmentally friendly soy based inks.

2. — 2005, *Orca Balsa Wall Hanging* ^{Design} / <u>FAUNA by Ross Menuez</u> ^{Manufacturer} / <u>AREAWARE</u> ^{Material} / Balsa wood tiles, cotton canvas, environmentally friendly soy based inks.

3. — 2005, *Camel Balsa Wall Hanging* ^{Design} / <u>FAUNA by Ross Menuez</u> ^{Manufacturer} / <u>AREAWARE</u> ^{Material} / Balsa wood, cotton canvas, environmentally friendly soy based inks.

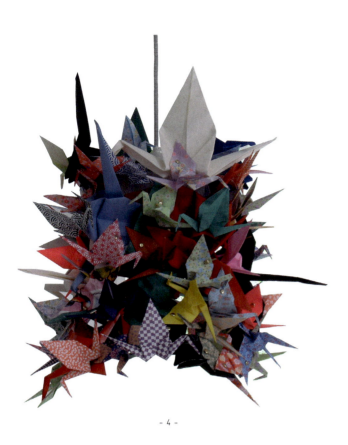

- 4 -

4. — **Tas-ka** 2007, *Birdshade Multicolour* ^{Design} / <u>Hester Worst, Jantien Baas</u> ^{Manufacturer} / <u>Tas-ka</u> ^{Material} / Paper ^{Description} / Folded paper cranes, suggesting a swarm of birds.

5 - 7. — **Frazier & Wing** 2008, *Bright Mix Mobile* ^{Design} / <u>Heather Frazier</u> ^{Manufacturer} / <u>Frazier & Wing</u> ^{Material} / Paper, acrylic, monofilament ^{Description} / Decorative mobile

- 5 -

- 6 -

- 7 -

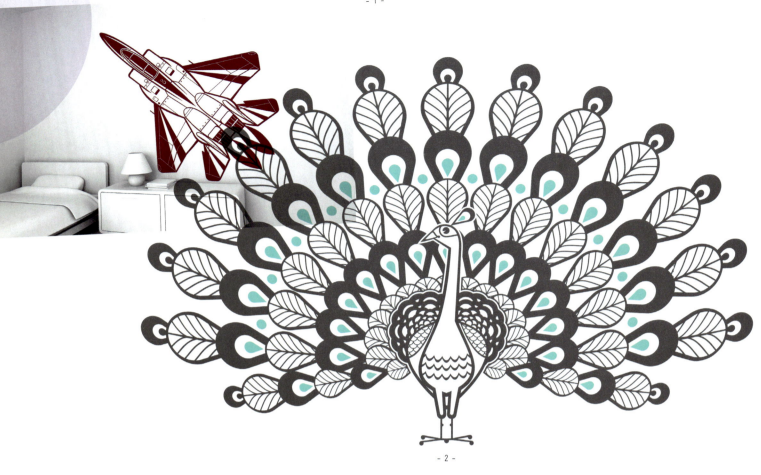

- 2 -

E-GLUE

Are childhood images universal around the globe? To what degree should we embrace or update the fabulous fairy tales of our youth? These are questions raised by designers Marielle Baldelli and Sébastien Messerschmidt of Lyon-based E-Glue, a studio specialising in concept and design for kids in the form of huge, colourful wall stickers.

Baldelli and Messerschmidt graduated from the National Higher School of Decorative Arts and founded E-Glue in 2007, launching products aimed at shaking up what they saw as a rigidly standardised world of kids' accessories and décor. The E-Glue approach is based on the notion that space is a blank page for illustration. And to them, illustration, on the proper scale (BIGGG), is a window on the imagination. It can transform any environment into a «narrative space» where mundane objects and surfaces are transmuted into adhesive vinyl characters like «Batchicky», the «Chicky Jazz Band» and «JoJo the Robot» and objects that seem to have personality in their own right: Cheerful sunflowers, monkeys and giraffes in scarlet, deep blues and chocolate browns. 'Characters from our childhood are obviously the starting point of our work but the goal is now to add our graphic and design research, which means creating our own identity,' says Messerschmidt. 'We realise that childhood imagery is pre-conditioned and that many parents don't dare to not uphold these "clichés". But we will continue to create products that are more personal, even if they are less successful for the moment.'

1. — **E-Glue** 2008, *Looping (giant wall sticker)* Design / Marielle Baldelli & Sébastien Messerschmidt Material / Adhesive vinyl.

2. — 2007, *Peacock (giant wall sticker)* Design / Marielle Baldelli & Sébastien Messerschmidt Material / Adhesive vinyl.

3. — 2007, *Princess castle (giant wall sticker)* Design / Marielle Baldelli & Sébastien Messerschmidt Material / Adhesive vinyl.

The couple injects its own graphic style to remake some of the classic tropes of delight and enchantment: Fire-red fire trucks and iconic castles, violet rocket ships and rats scurrying up the rigging of pirate ship poop decks, peacocks in green-and-yellow or black and celadon green. The work makes various references, drawing from very different cultures, as well as different artistic disciplines, including cartoons, movies, interior and web design, decorative arts, architecture, typography, graphic design, illustration and the visual arts. Baldelli and Messerschmidt's «Little Piece of Heaven» is an interchangeable set of wall stickers: A treehouse with a tiny garden of sunflowers, birds delivering a love letter, a cat chasing a butterfly at the foot of the tree, a horse watering the flowers with his tail. There's «Looping», a purple jet fighter or «Lovely Uma!» With Kipling-esque animals; a giraffe, lion, monkey and elephant. There are sheriff-cacti and shrimps bigger than lobsters. The «Tutti Frutti» scene features a sloth and a wallaby amid kudzu vines. E-Glue's giant wall sticker «Tyrannosaurus rex» isn't just standing around like a natural history museum exhibit, it's a roaring skeleton.

'On the face of it, childhood imagery seems to be universal,' says Baldelli. E-Glue has found customers around the globe, from the US, Australia, Europe and the Middle East to South Africa and South America. But what these buyers have in common is their interest in design, graphics and illustration. In fact, they often work in the visual arts, most of them in design or at communications agencies. 'Adults offer our products to their kids because they appreciate our work,' says Messerschmidt, 'but there are also a few adults who buy it for themselves.'

4. — 2008, *Hummingbirds (giant wall sticker)* Design / Marielle Baldelli & Sébastien Messerschmidt Material / Adhesive vinyl.

5. — 2007, *Lovely Uma! (decor set of wall stickers)* Design / Marielle Baldelli & Sébastien Messerschmidt Material / Adhesive vinyl.

- 1 -

- 2 -

1. — **E-Glue** 2007, *Hut for birds (giant wall sticker)* ^{Design} / Marielle Baldelli & Sébastien Messerschmidt ^{Material} / Adhesive vinyl.

2. — 2007, *Sheriff cactus (giant wall sticker)* ^{Design} / Marielle Balcelli & Sébastien Messerschmidt ^{Material} / Adhesive vinyl.

3. — 2007, *Giga-KIT // boarding ! (decor set of wall stickers)* ^{Design} / Marielle Baldelli & Sébastien Messerschmidt ^{Material} / Adhesive vinyl.

4. — 2008, *E-Glue // adhesive design for kids* ^{Design} / Marielle Baldelli & Sébastien Messerschmidt ^{Material} / Adhesive vinyl.

- 3 -

- 4 -

5. — 2008, *Little Piece of Heaven (decor set of wall stickers)*
Design / <u>Marielle Baldelli & Sébastien Messerschmidt</u> Material / Adhesive vinyl.

6. — 2007, *Excavator (giant wall sticker)* Design / <u>Marielle Baldelli &</u>
<u>Sébastien Messerschmidt</u> Material / Adhesive vinyl.

7. — 2007, *Fire! Fire! (giant wall sticker)* Design / <u>Marielle Baldelli &</u>
<u>Sébastien Messerschmidt</u> Material / Adhesive vinyl.

1. — **Wee Gallery** 2007, *Sea Wall Graphics* ^{Design} / <u>Surya Sajnani</u> ^{Manufacturer} / <u>Wee Gallery</u> ^{Material} / Polypropylene.

2. — 2004, *Photo Mobile with Wee Gallery Cards* ^{Design} / <u>Wil Van Den Bos</u> ^{Photography} / <u>Christian Lunardi</u> ^{Manufacturer} / <u>Kikkerland</u> ^{Material} / Stainless steel.

3. — 2004, *Giraffe Wall Graphics* ^{Design} / <u>Surya Sajnani</u> ^{Manufacturer} / <u>Wee Gallery</u> ^{Material} / Polypropylene.

- 1 -

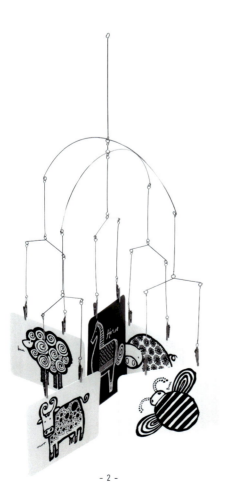

- 2 -

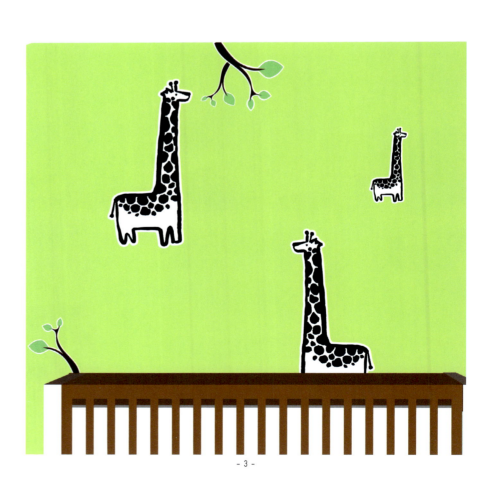

- 3 -

1. — **Boodalee** 2007, *Boodalee 'Space' Wall Graphics and Bedding* ^{Design} / <u>Boodalee</u> ^{Photography} / <u>Mark Adams</u> ^{Manufacturer} / <u>Boo-dalee</u> ^{Material} / Bedding: 250 thread count, 100% cotton percale. Wall Graphics: Made of self-adhesive matte vinyl, the wall decals are easily removable.

2. — 2008, *Trees Wall Graphics in White* ^{Design} / <u>Boodalee</u> ^{Photography} / <u>Mark Adams</u> ^{Manufacturer} / <u>Boodalee by blik</u> ^{Material} / Self-adhesive vinyl wall graphics.

3. — 2008 (wall graphics) 2007 (bedding), *Boodalee's City Collection* ^{Design} / <u>Boodalee</u> ^{Photography} / <u>Mark Adams</u> ^{Manufacturer} / <u>Boodalee</u> (bedding) <u>Boodalee by blik</u> (wall graphics) ^{Material} / Bedding: 250 thread count, 100% cotton percale. Wall Graphics: Self adhesive, vinyl.

- 1 -

- 2 -

- 3 -

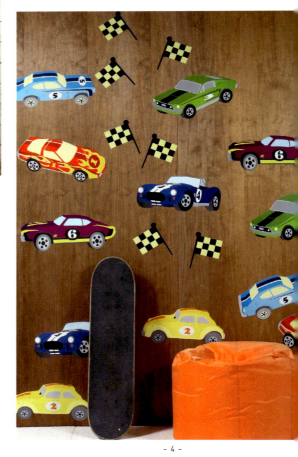

- 4 -

1. — **WallCandy Arts** 2008, *Candy Factory* Design / WallCandy
Material / Removable non-toxic wall art / decoration.

2. — 2008, *Stripes Blue* Design / WallCandy
Material / Removable non-toxic wall art / decoration.

3. — 2008, *Deerly Beloved* Design / WallCandy
Material / Removable non-toxic wall art / decoration.

4. — 2008, *Stripes Blue* Design / Rad Racers
Material / Removable non-toxic wall art / decoration.

- 5 -

5. — **WallCandy Arts** 2008, *Flutterflies* ^{Design} / <u>WallCandy</u> ^{Material} / Removable non-toxic wall art / decoration.

6. — 2008, *DottiLicious* ^{Design} / <u>WallCandy</u>
^{Material} / Removable non-toxic wall art / decoration.

7. — 2008, *Transport* ^{Design} / Rad Racers
^{Material} / Removable non-toxic wall art / decoration.

8. — 2008, *Grazeland* ^{Design} / <u>WallCandy</u>
^{Material} / Removable non-toxic wall art / decoration.

- 7 -

- 6 -

- 8 -

EXPLORATION

Children never stop noticing what is going around them. And they are even more sociable and sensitive when outside of their known environments. Be it while travelling, visiting restaurants or simply accompanying their parents to exhibitions, children are curious and inquisitive all the time, trying to understand new forms and expanses, thus gaining access to the adult world.

EXPLORATION presents new spaces and innovative temporary experiences for children that mediate between children and the phenomena they perceive beyond playgrounds, school and home.

The projects presented here help to shape the kids' visual senses, including the manner in which they experience form and surface as well as how they can intervene and playfully register them. It is only when they discover all those hidden meanings and pre-defined concepts that they are able to - if not change them - then at least to question them.

A forward-thinking example of this approach is Dutch eating designer Marije Vogelzang's project for a paediatrics clinic in New York that treats obese kids with serious food addictions. Fighting obesity means completely changing a person's attitude towards eating. Consequently, for this project Vogelzang disregarded the healthy-versus-unhealthy dichotomy. She designed a series of colour-coded snacks based on a philosophy that attributes certain hues to the development of certain skills; e.g. red treats being a source of self-confidence, yellow nibbles promoting the ability to make friends, and so on. The concept helped pave the route to recovery.

Furthermore, EXPLORATION presents museums for children that address children in special ways (for example via new media and music), hotels that have been designed to be more suitable for children (with the calculated side effect that their parents might also stay longer…) as well as restaurants that give kids the opportunity to eat food in a way that is joyous and healthy alike. Projects like that of Brooklyn-based designer Chris Woebken go even further. When she found a website detailing the extrasensory perceptions of animals, the Animal Superpowers project was born. Using microscopes, electronics, plastic and plywood, she teamed up with Kenichi Okada to create an experimental series of toys that serve as sensory enhancements as much as they are biology edutainment: "As the first experiment," Woebken recalls, "I tried building a mock-up of an insect vision device out of a welding mask, a screen and a microscope mounted to a walking stick." Then they began to build more tools that would allow humans to experience the extraordinary senses of various animals, taking each to the park for testing by curious local kids.

Curiosity might have killed some cats but it surely enlivens the kids who, fuelled by it, take it as an invitation to explore the world around them.

pp. 166 – 193

4

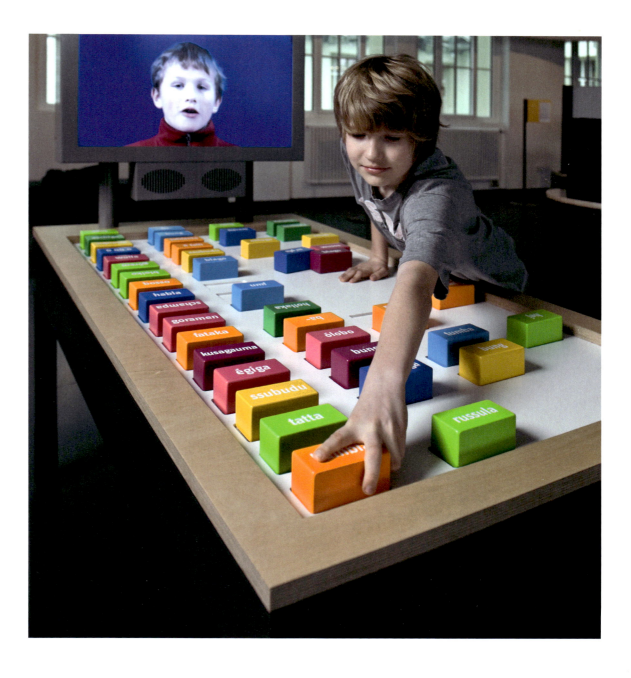

François Azambourg 2007, *Workshop for children*, Villa Noailles

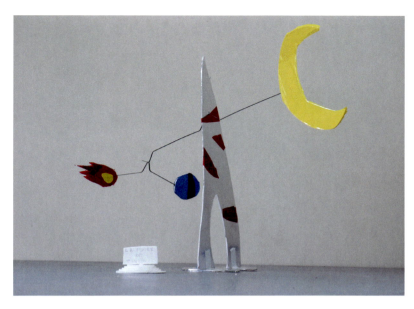

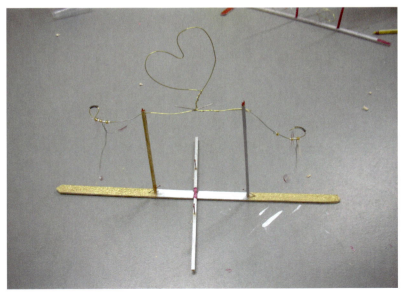

FULGURO

Design studio Fulguro is Yves Fidalgo and Cédric Decroux. They joined forces while studying at the Ecole cantonale d'art de Lausanne. Based in Lausanne, Switzerland, they have worked since 2001 across a range of disciplines which include furniture, product and graphic design.

The idea for the Ateliers pour Enfants in Villa Noailles was to have children work with digital cameras and get more familiar with the technical aspects including exposure time, diaphragm and framing: "Each time we tried to give them a new exercise/ theme to work on so that it would complete their knowledge of the photographic tool." It all started when The Villa Noailles asked the Swiss designers to run workshops for children:

"We don't have vast experience in teaching, but in these type of workshops the goals for children and adults are quite different. One of the things we asked the children to do was to take pictures of things in and around the Villa Noailles in order to make an alphabet. They found many examples of shapes in the architecture and in nature and were able to represent every letter from A to Z." Still, the project didn't run by itself. "Kids are quite unpredictable. They are passionate about something for a moment and a moment later they couldn't care less. It was a real challenge to keep them focussed for three hours. Each atelier was held on one afternoon. Each time we gave them new instructions and they had to do the project in the afternoon. It didn't work all the time..."

- 1 -

- 2 -

1 + 2. — **Fulguro (Yves Fidalgo & Cédric Decroux)** 2005 - 2006, *Workshop for children*, Villa Noailles ᴬʳᵗⁱˢᵗ / Professors: <u>Joël Tettamanti & Fulguro</u> ᴾʰᵒᵗᵒᵍʳᵃᵖʰʸ / <u>The kids</u> ᴹᵃᵗᵉʳⁱᵃˡ / Camera, tripod ᴰᵉˢᶜʳⁱᵖᵗⁱᵒⁿ / Photography workshop for children. Workshop n. 6 – setup: Two cameras facing each other. Each camera takes a picture so that both sides, front and back, reveal something different.

- 3 -

- 4 -

- 5 -

- 6 -

3 - 5. — 2005 - 2006, *Workshop for children*, Villa Noailles ᴬʳᵗⁱˢᵗ / <u>Profes-seurs: Joël Tettamanti & Fulguro</u> ᴾʰᵒᵗᵒᵍʳᵃᵖʰʸ / <u>The kids</u> ᴹᵃᵗᵉʳⁱᵃˡ / Camera, tri-pod ᴰᵉˢᶜʳⁱᵖᵗⁱᵒⁿ / Workshop n. 1: Place the camera. To define a cropping space in the room use a thin cord. Stage yourself and play with the frame of the picture.

6 + 7. — 2005 - 2006, *Workshop for children*, Villa Noailles ᴬʳᵗⁱˢᵗ / <u>Profes-seurs: Joël Tettamanti & Fulguro</u> ᴾʰᵒᵗᵒᵍʳᵃᵖʰʸ / <u>The kids</u> ᴹᵃᵗᵉʳⁱᵃˡ / Camera, tri-pod ᴰᵉˢᶜʳⁱᵖᵗⁱᵒⁿ / Workshop n. 3: To cut images out of magazines and display them within the shot. Play with the fore- and background.

- 7 -

1. — **Fulguro** 2005 - 2006, *Workshop for children*, Villa Noailles ^{Artist} / Professeurs: Joël Tettamanti & Fulguro ^{Photography} / The kids ^{Material} / Camera ^{Description} / Workshop n. 2: Using photography, create an illusion, a magic trick.

2. — 2005 - 2006, *Workshop for children*, Villa Noailles ^{Artist} / Professeurs: Joël Tettamanti & Fulguro ^{Photography} / The kids ^{Material} / Camera, tripod ^{Description} / Atelier 2: Par la photo, créer une illusion, un tour de magie.

3. — 2005 - 2006, *Workshop for children*, Villa Noailles ^{Artist} / Professeurs: Joël Tettamanti & Fulguro ^{Photography} / The kids ^{Material} / Camera, tripod ^{Description} / Workshop n. 1: Place the camera. To define a cropping space in the room use a thin cord. Stage yourself and play with the frame of the picture.

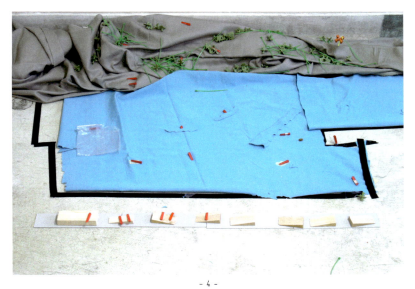

- 4 -

- 6 -

- 5 -

- 7 -

4 - 7. — **Fulguro** 2005 - 2006, *Workshop for children*, Villa Noailles ^Artist / Professeurs: Joël Tettamanti & Fulguro ^Photography / The kids ^Material / Camera, tripod ^Description / Workshop n.5: Using heterogeneous materials and reproduce images from famous photographers (Andreas Gursky, Bern or Hilla Becher).

John Morgan studio 2004, *Behind the Glass: Voices of White City*
Design / John Morgan studio   Material / Glass, window cleaner, stencils, brushes   Description / Children's workshop. The BBC comissioned a visual solution to a one-day writing workshop held by author Vivian French. Texts were applied by children and parents onto glass using stencils, brushes and Windolene (a window cleaning product). Reminiscent of Tom Sawyer and The Fence.

- 1 -

1 + 2. — **Marine Duroselle** 2007, *Ayacucho* ^Photography^ / Marine Duroselle ^Description^ / Picture taken during the carnival of Ayacucho (Peru).

3. — **Adrien Rovero** 2008, *Flying Object | Workshop at the Villa Noailles* ^Photography^ / Adrien Rovero ^Material^ / Styrofoam, balloon, helium ^Description^ / The idea was to design a flying object made out of Styrofoam. All kids received a balloon full of helium and had to create an object. At the end of the workshop, a station was build to drop all the balloons at once.

- 2 -

- 3 -

Adrien Rovero 2008, *Flying Object | Workshop at the Villa Noailles*   Photography / <u>Adrien Rovero</u>   Material / Styrofoam, balloon, helium   Description / Children had to design a flying object made out Styrofoam. All kids received a balloon full of helium and had to create an object. Project were related to the fact that a message can be written. At the end of the workshop, a station was built to drop all the balloons at once.

Adrien Rovero 2008, *la cabane pot de fleurs / Objets carlets | Workshop at the Villa Noailles* Photography / Adrien Rovero Material / Wood Description / During the courses, kids explored objects and construction through little beams. They first worked on a scale of 1:10 and then translated it into a scale of 1:1. The result is a series of scaled furniture made out of wood, glue and screws. In addition to having an actual object at the end of the courses, they initiated a design process with drawings, scale models, development and prototypes.

Jordi Ferreiro is a graphic designer from Barcelona who has also worked as an art educator in museums and art centres during previous years. His «Floating Exhibition» workshop for children is aimed at "making them lose fear of museums and art as if it was something sacred and distant. It also attempts to explain the difference between a museum and an art centre in a playful manner. It is a reflection about the use of our daily space and what we make of it." Realising this project had a huge impact on Ferreiro's own work:

"The experience was amazing. Previously, I was a geometric artist; really obsessed with the perfection form and colour. After working with kids, my interest is still formalist but without the pressure of perfection and with more interest in the process and the collaboration. There is no doubt that kids explore the materials and the ideas with a 100% capacity, and the results can be magic for them. Adults, on the other hand, work with the intention of making a good work, using concepts or techniques that they know will function, but they usually don´t really explore that much."

At best it was a rich experience for his collaborators as well: "I hope they learned to use their own resources to do whatever they want within their limitations and to express themselves with art.

JORDI FERREIRO

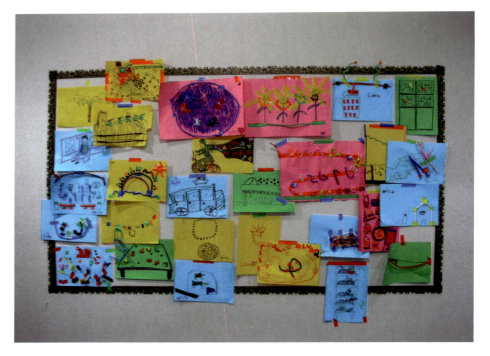

Jordi Ferreiro 2008, *A Floating Exhibition*
Design /Jordi Ferreiro   Material / Colour balloons
Description / Pedagogic workshop for kids.

Jordi Ferreiro 2008, *A Floating Exhibition*
Design / Jordi Ferreiro   Material / Colour balloons
Description / Pedagogic workshop for kids.

- 1 -

- 2 -

- 3 -

1. — **Jordi Ferreiro** 2008 *A Floating Exhibition (on the beach!)*
Material / Colour balloons   Description / Pedagogic workshop for kids.

2. — 2007, *Art in the Space workshop*   Material / Tape
Description / Pedagogic workshop with kids.

3 + 4. — 2008, *Artist book laboratory*   Material / Books and art stuff
Description / Pedagogic workshop with kids.

- 4 -

- 2 -

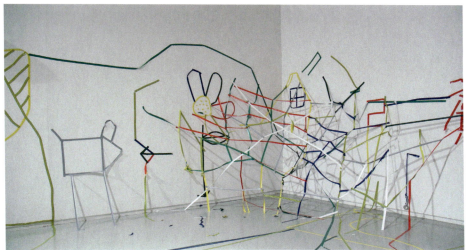

Jordi Ferreiro 2007 *Art in the Space workshop*
Material / Tape   Description / Pedagogic workshop with kids.

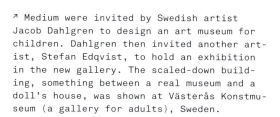

↗ Medium were invited by Swedish artist Jacob Dahlgren to design an art museum for children. Dahlgren then invited another artist, Stefan Edqvist, to hold an exhibition in the new gallery. The scaled-down building, something between a real museum and a doll's house, was shown at Västerås Konstmuseum (a gallery for adults), Sweden.

Medium 2007-2008, *Barnens Konstmuseum*
Design / Jacob Dahlgren and Medium   Photography / Felix Bruggemann

CHRIS WOEBKEN
&
KENICHI OKADA

Crickets listen with their legs, falcons see in sharp focus even while diving at 100 miles per hour. A catfish has 10 times as many taste buds than a human being. An octopus has a rectangular pupil but a penguin's cornea is flat. Seahorses can move each eye independently, but scorpions have up to a dozen eyes; spiders only have eight.

When Brooklyn designer Chris Woebken found a website detailing the extrasensory perceptions of animals, the Animal Superpowers project was born. Using microscopes, electronics, plastic and plywood, the former IDEO employee teamed up with fellow Royal College of Art graduate Kenichi Okada to create an experimental series of toys that serve as sensory enhancements as much as they provide biology edutainment. 'For the first experiment,' Woebken recalls, 'I tried building a mock-up insect vision device out of a welding mask, a screen and a microscope mounted to a walking stick.' Then the designing duo began to build more tools that would allow humans to experience the extraordinary senses of various animals, taking each to the park for testing by curious local kids.

Woebken and Okada's three working prototypes include an ant apparatus that magnifies the wearer's vision by 50 times through handheld microscope antennas, suddenly enabling a person to perceive unprecedented surface detail. 'It allows you to «see» through your hands,' Woebken says, 'and to dive into a secret, previously hidden world.' Their bird device recreates a bird's sense of direction via a head-mounted solenoid compass that exploits Global Positioning System technology to vibrate when its wearer is oriented in a certain predetermined direction. It functions by approximating a bird's detection of geomagnetic fields in order to wing its way south in the winter and north again in the spring. The giraffe device acts, in Woebken's words, 'as a child-to-adult converter' by shifting the wearer's voice to lower octaves and raising one's eye-level by 30 centimetres.

'Rather than enhancing the functional aspects of products, I'm interested in designing new sensory experiences in relation to things that are normally invisible

- 1 -

1. — **Chris Woebken** 2008, *Animal Superpowers - Ant Device*
Design / <u>Chris Woebken & Kenichi Okada</u>
Material / Microscope, electronics, plastics.

2. — 2008, *Ant Device* Design / <u>Chris Woebken & Kenichi Okada</u>
Material / Electronics, plastics, plywood.

to us,' Woebken explains. 'Kenichi and I tried to create tools to re-imagine the human relationship to animals by providing a new lens, a view from the animal perspective. And adults actually enjoy those toys very much as well.'

The senses evolved to equip humans and other animals with crucial survival tools: Elephants sense an approaching tsunami by hearing low frequencies that humans aren't able to detect. Ants communicate through smell. By studying natural systems and biomimetics, an increasing number of designers like Woebken and Okada can help children (and attentive parents) understand how humans may need to change in order to get in synch with both our technology and the world in which we live.

The Animal Superpowers project led to the construction of a «beetle wrestling robot» that allows its user to pit himself against the strongest animal in the world and a «bat billboard» that re-imagines human interactions with wild animals in an urban setting. And the evolution continues …

- 2 -

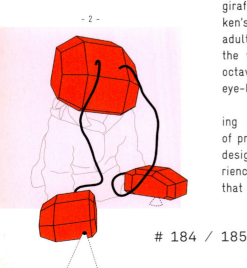

- 3 -

3. — 2008, *Animal Superpowers - Animals in the Park*
Design / <u>Chris Woebken & Kenichi Okada</u> Material / Electronics, plastic, plywood.

4. — 2008, *Bird Device* Design / <u>Chris Woebken & Kenichi Okada</u>
Material / Electronics, plastics.

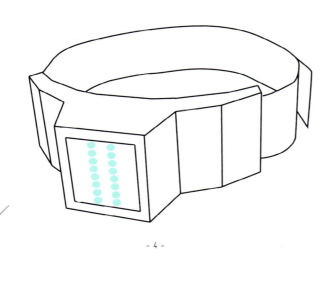

- 4 -

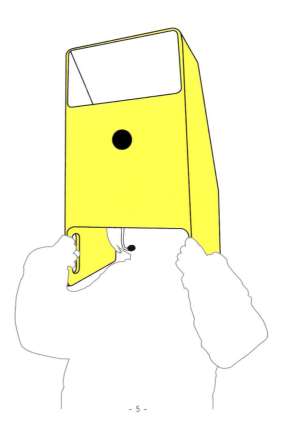

- 5 -

5. — 2008, *Giraffe Device* Design / <u>Chris Woebken & Kenichi Okada</u>
Material / Electronics, plywood.

6. — 2008, *Animals in the park* Design / <u>Chris Woebken & Kenichi Okada</u>
Material / Electronics, plastic, plywood.

- 6 -

Hubertus Wald Kinderreich 2008, *Garten der Dinge.*

HUBERTUS
WALD
KINDERREICH

Hubertus Wald Kinderreich is funded by the charitable, Hamburg-based Hubertus Wald foundation, which was founded in 1993. The foundation is subdivided in two departments, one focussing on medical support and one focussing on the support of selected cultural projects. Being temporarily set up within the building of Hamburg's Museum für Kunst und Gewerbe (Museum for Art and Trade), Hubertus Wald Kinderreich is an interactive design museum for kids. This adventurous space provides a multitude of opportunities for children to learn and discover the «design of things».

They can engage in the exploration of the essence and form of the material world just like architects, designers and artists. Instead of just being passive observers here, they are encouraged to craft objects out of porcelain, illustrate posters or textiles, re-design and re-enact historical and fictitious situations at their height. This museum is not only the first one of its kind, but deservedly called a museum for applied arts.

1. — **studio klv** 2008, *The Speed of Nature*   ^{Design} / studio klv   ^{Photography} / Axl Klein   ^{Manufacturer} / Trillian Gesellschaft für mediale Lösungen mbH   ^{Description} / Running, crawling, jumping. This is where kids can suss out all the secrets of the natural world.

2. — 2008, *Flight Paths*   ^{Design} / studio klv   ^{Photography} / Axl Klein   ^{Manufacturer} / Trillian Gesellschaft für mediale Lösungen mbH   ^{Description} / Pitching curves helps to discover which path a ball takes when thrown into the air diagonally.

3. — 2008, *Footrace*   ^{Design} / studio klv   ^{Photography} / Axl Klein   ^{Manufacturer} / Trillian Gesellschaft für mediale Lösungen mbH   ^{Description} / Run as fast as an animal and step onto the track when you seen an animal you would like to race!

4. — 2008, *Hovering Ball*   ^{Design} / studio klv   ^{Photography} / Axl Klein   ^{Manufacturer} / Trillian Gesellschaft für mediale Lösungen mbH   ^{Description} / Cranking it into the air, how can you get the ball to hover?

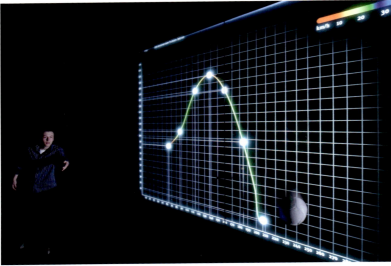

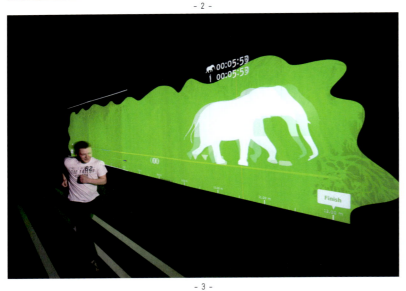

- 5 -

- 6 -

5. — 2007, *Jump Analysis* ^{Design} / studio klv ^{Photography} / Axl Klein ^{Manufacturer} / Trillian Gesellschaft für mediale Lösungen mbH ^{Description} / Record the highlight. What does the highest point of your jump look like?

6. — 2008, *Coaxing the rope snakes* ^{Design} / studio klv ^{Photography} / Axl Klein ^{Manufacturer} / Trillian Gesellschaft für mediale Lösungen mbH ^{Description} / What shapes does the rope make in the air? Alter the position of the lever carefully. You can play with the rope diverting its course by using your hand or an object.

- 8 -

- 7 -

7. — 2007, *Poem Generator* ^{Design} / studio klv ^{Photography} / Axl Klein ^{Manufacturer} / Trillian Gesellschaft für mediale Lösungen mbH

8. — 2008, *Curved Slides* ^{Design} / studio klv ^{Photography} / Axl Klein ^{Manufacturer} / Trillian Gesellschaft für mediale Lösungen mbH ^{Description} / The quickest way round. Who is first? Start at the same time to slide your way down the slide. The person on the curved slide reaches the end first. The time needed to reach the finishing line doesn't just depend on the distance, but also the speed at which something or someone travels.

- 1 -

1. (Top) — **Marije Vogelzang | Proef** 2007, *Veggie bling bling*
Description / Making bling bling with veggies using childrens teeth
as a shaping tool makes them EAT CARROTS!! (Model: Juni)

2. — 2007, *Veggie bling bling*.

3. — 2007, *Veggie bling bling*.

- 4 -

- 2 -

- 3 -

4. — 2007, *Chocola d'amour* Description / Lisette with a chocolate mustache.

5. — 2007, *Chocola d'amour*.

- 5 -

6. — 2007, *Veggie bling bling.*

7. — *Plant Wear*
Description / Green Sprouts Hat (Model: Marije).

MARIJE VOGELZANG

Marije Vogelzang is not a food designer. She is a Dutch product designer who graduated from the Design Academy Eindhoven and chose to use food as her main material because of her love for it.

The mother of a four-year old daughter knows quite well how to communicate with children in an educational manner. This includes, for example, a playful way of getting children to eat vegetables - voluntarily! She invited kids from the day-care centre next door to her restaurant Proef in Amsterdam for an indoor picnic. By simply encouraging them to use their teeth as a shaping tool to create what she calls «veggie bling bling» - which automatically made them eat carrots, among other things - she almost turned them into aficionados of raw vegetables.

Another example of Vogelzang's unorthodox approach is a project from 2003 for a paediatrics clinic in New York that treats obese kids with serious food addictions. In most cases, getting to the root of such an obsession takes more than a diet featuring healthy snacks. Fighting obesity means completely changing a person's attitude towards eating. Consequently, for this project, Vogelzang disregarded the healthy-versus-unhealthy dichotomy. She designed a series of colour-coded snacks based on a philosophy that attributes certain hues to the development of certain skills. Red treats are a source of self-confidence, yellow nibbles promote the ability to make friends, and black

- 1 -

snacks help the child to practice self-discipline. In the eyes of the kids, the wholesome ingredients that go into this food are largely irrelevant. The concept helped pave the route to recovery.

If that is not already music to every nutritionist's ear, then Marije spills the beans on another concept: "An old English children's song says «Beans beans the musical fruit, the more you eat the more you toot, beans are good for your heart. The more you eat the more you fart.» This is my attempt to sell more jars of beans to children by just changing the label on the jar. Eventually this can lead to national farting contests or a farting orchestra!"

1. — **Marije Vogelzang | Proef** 2006, *Kinderen Sam Sam*
Description / Indoor picnic at Proef with the children of the neighbouring daycare centre at in the park.

2. — *Plant Wear* Description / *How to make your kid into a green monster.*

(garden) cress–dress

geraspte kaas eroverheen

boterhammetje tuinkers

tuinkersnaam of borsthaar ''

koksmuts

maak van je kind een groen monster of een egel

tuinkers als grote plant ook lekker! (minder gezond...)

dit is een grote lap stof

- 1 -

- 2 -

- 3 -

- 4 -

3. — 2007, *Chocola d'amour* ^{Description} / 'Sandwich with sausage'.

4. — 2007, '*Beans beans the musical fruit*, the more you eat the more you toot, beans are good for your heart. The more you eat the more you fart'.

5. — 2007, *Chocola d'amour* ^{Description} / Chocolate wall at Chocola d' amour.

6. — 2007, *Toothless candybox* ^{Description} / Toothless candybox 'do-it-yourself' How horrible it would feel if you don't have teeth and you always have to eat with your false teeth. Let's just lie on the couch, take your teeth out and enjoy a box full of powders, melts and liquid candy. Children can make this themselves for grandma, grandpa or anyone without teeth.

7. — 2007, *Monkey ears from bread* (Marije).

- 5 -

- 7 -

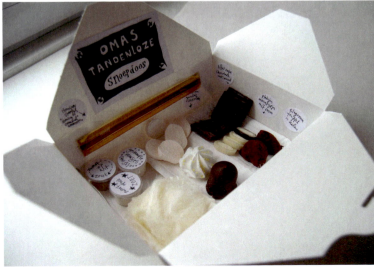

- 6 -

EXPRESS YOURSELF

Kids love to play games and they love to play role games even more. Putting on a mask, dressing up or behaving like a different character to disguise your identity or to change it is perhaps the most primal and natural instinct a child has. The fact of the matter is, it doesn't hide the child's identity but helps to shape and explore it. Playing with identity enables children to find out who they are, respectively who they want to become, and how they are viewed by others. They will be more daring and self-confident once they have realised their fantasy and dressed themselves accordingly. Also, in refusing to wear the fashion style (and brands) preferred by their parents, the kid strengthens its personality and imagination.

> Expressing yourself means to define yourself, means being able to distinguish yourself from others.

Children emancipate themselves from clichés (pink is for girls and blue for boys…) by taking designated items and clothing out of their context and combining them in new ways. Not caring about clichés is of course a lesson that is learned quickly this way. Sometimes a kid's buddies might tease him about the latest combination of those silver boots and the elder brother's oversized anorak, but this just means that the kid learns as much about the expectations of others as it learns about self-perception. How does this affect me and others? Will I put this on again despite the teasing? Or do they have a point and I really do look a little silly? More significant yet, is the fact that the kid also learns about friends, parents and people by noticing their comments (or the absence of comments!).

> EXPRESS YOURSELF shows the whole range of possibilities within this highly entertaining and creative field of design for children, ranging from well-designed everyday clothes to unique accessories and costumes for special occasions along with projects from designers and photographers that take up on the aforementioned fantasies and ideas as inspirations and impulses for playful projects and creations. Take, for instance, the Dutch photographer Jan von Holleben: "I see that kids are very easy to play with and to photograph. They are natural and not disturbed by thinking too much about the photographical aspect that depicts them as individuals. I am trying to not put too much focus on the photograph when shooting, but rather focus on the game that we play and its success. I am always trying to create a real image that takes reality to another level and eventually I want the viewer to focus on that more profound level. This is fun for me and for them… and that does the trick. When I was a kid I loved playing and spent hours and days with friends and family playing all sorts of games. Here I am today doing exactly the same thing that I used to do as a child; now, as a grown up, it even includes an intellectual level that satisfies me. Sometimes I am gobsmacked by the possibilities and adventures that I see in the far distance on the horizon where my horse gallops to take me there…
> sooner or later!"

5

- 1 -

- 2 -

- 3 -

Opposite page — **Delphine Chanet** 2005, *Appoline*
Photography / <u>Delphine Chanet</u>   Material / Photo   Description / Editorial project.

1. — 2005, *Ondine*   Photography / <u>Delphine Chanet</u>
Manufacturer / <u>Milk Magazine</u>   Material / Photo   Description / Editorial project.

2. — 2004, *Thaïs*   Photography / <u>Delphine Chanet</u>   Material / Photo.

3. — 2008, *Lubies*   Photography / <u>Delphine Chanet</u>
Manufacturer / <u>Milk Magazine</u>   Material / Photo   Description / Editorial project.

4. — 2005, *Ours*   Photography / <u>Delphine Chanet</u>   Material / Photo
Description / Editorial project.

- 4 -

Jan von Holleben 2008, *Monster*
Photography / <u>Jan von Holleben</u> Material / Photo.

JAN VON HOLLEBEN

Brought up in the Southern German countryside, von Holleben lived most of his youth in an alternative commune environment. At the age of 13 he followed his father's photographic career by picking up a camera and experimenting with all sorts of «magical» tricks, constantly developing his photographic skills with friends and family. After his graduation at the Surrey Institute of Art and Design, he became immersed in the London photographic scene, where he quickly set up two photographic collectives, became involved as picture editor and photographic director for magazines and agencies, and won several prestigious awards each year with his own photography. For some of his work, Jan von Holleben, whose mother was a child therapist, involves his local neighbourhood kids and their friends with his playful and adventurous ideas:

1. — **Jan von Holleben** 2004, *The Diver*   Photography / Jan von Holleben   Material / Photo.

2. — 2002, *The Dog Rider*   Photography / Jan von Holleben   Material / Photo.

"I see that kids are very easy to play with and to photograph. They are natural and not disturbed by thinking too much about the photographical aspect that depicts them as individuals. I am trying to not put too much focus on the photograph when shooting pictures, but rather focus on the game that we play and to succeed at it. I am always trying to create a real image that takes reality to another level and eventually I want the viewer to focus on that second level. This is fun for me and for them … and that does the trick.

When I was a kid I loved playing and spent hours and days with friends and family playing all sorts of games. Here I am today doing exactly the same thing that I used to do as a child; now, as a grown up, it even includes an intellectual level that satisfies me. Sometimes I am gobsmacked by the possibilities and adventures that I see in the far distance on the horizon where my horse gallops to take me there… sooner or later!"

«Dreams of Flying» is his most acclaimed photographic project to date.

3. — 2004, *The Tarzan and Jan* ^{Photography} / <u>Jan von Holleben</u> ^{Material} / Photo.

4. — 2004, *The Gardener* ^{Photography} / <u>Jan von Holleben</u> ^{Material} / Photo.

5. — 2004, *The Race* ^{Photography} / <u>Jan von Holleben</u> ^{Material} / Photo.

1. (Left) — **LULA** 2008, *Petit Magazine*
Photography / <u>Elisabeth Dunker</u> Description / Fashion job (styling + photography) for Petit Magazine.

2. — 2008, *Small Magazine*
Photography / <u>Elisabeth Dunker</u> Description / Fashion job (styling + photography) for Small Magazine.

3. — 2008, *Cover photo*
Photography / <u>Elisabeth Dunker</u> Description / Fashion job (styling + photography) for Petit Magazine.

4. — 2008, *Petit Magazine*
Photography / <u>Elisabeth Dunker</u> Description / Fashion job (styling + photography) for Petit Magazine.

- 2 -

- 3 -

- 4 -

- 1 -

- 3 -

1. — **Aymara** 2008, *Knitted cardigan Pooh and hand knit hat* ^{Styling} / <u>Yannina Esquivias</u>
^{Photography} / <u>Diego Franssens</u> ^{Manufacturer} / <u>Aymara</u> ^{Material} / Baby alpaca.

2. — 2008, *Hand made scarf with pompoms Lore and knitted cardigan* ^{Styling} / <u>Yannina Esquivias</u>
^{Photography} / <u>Diego Franssens</u> ^{Manufacturer} / <u>Aymara</u> ^{Material} / Baby alpaca.

3. — 2008, *Hand crocheted dress Olivia* ^{Styling} / <u>Yannina Esquivias</u>
^{Photography} / <u>Diego Franssens</u> ^{Manufacturer} / <u>Aymara</u> ^{Material} / Peruvian pima cotton.

- 2 -

Bureau Mario Lombardo 2007, *Silk scarf N° 4 + 5*
Design / Tania Parovic, Bureau Mario Lombardo
Photography / Markus Mrugalla   Material / Silk
Description / Design for the LittleRedRidingHood label.

- 1 -

- 2 -

1. — **Company** 2007, *Pinguwear* ^{Design} / Company (Aamu Song & Johan Olin) ^{Manufacturer} / Company.

2. — 2007, *Dance Shoes* ^{Design} / Company (Aamu Song & Johan Olin) ^{Material} / Felt ^{Manufacturer} / Company ^{Description} / Dance shoes for father and daughter.

3. — 2007, *Hood Bag* ^{Design} / Company (Aamu Song & Johan Olin).

4. — 2006, *Pferdhosen / Riding Pants* ^{Design} / Company (Aamu Song & Johan Olin) ^{Manufacturer} / Company ^{Material} / Leather ^{Description} / Riding pants for father and child.

- 3 -

- 4 -

Company 2005, *Spatial Dress*
Design / Company (Aamu Song & Johan Olin)
Manufacturer / Company   Description / A dress for all busy moms.

- 1 -

- 1 -

1 + 2. — **UniPHORMS** 2007, *Egypt, Submarine*
Design / Swantje Ziegler   Illustration / Susanne Asheuer   Photography / Stefan
Kraul   Manufacturer / UniPHORMS GmbH   Description / School Fashion.

UNIPHORMS

3 - 5. — 2007, *Treasure, Outer Space, Boat*
Design / Swantje Ziegler Illustration / Susanne Asheuer Photography / Stefan Kraul
Manufacturer / UniPHORMS GmbH
Description / School Fashion.

Uniforms are associated with bad connotations when mentioned in the same breath as school and children. Wrongly so. Instead of oppressing a kid's individuality, they can help to expose the very same, since they blot out everything that could blur character and personality. The vital proof that school (or kindergarten) uniforms don't have to look like the ones you know from old British TV series goes by the name of UniPHORMS. The company that was founded by fashion designer Swantje Ziegler and Dr. Alexander Olek in 2007 designs convenient, individual and functional clothing for use in schools that are tailored to meet the demands and ideas of children, their parents and the schools. This includes workshops where ideas are developed and discussed until they are ready to be produced in small manufactories.

As a result, these clothes are identical but still leave room for a kid's self-expression, while enabling them to concentrate on important things. The UniPHORMS' vision is "to enrich school's everyday life, to abolish social distinctions and to let a fresh breeze blow through the classrooms." The people who work for UniPHORMS are specialists in the fields of design, crop design, production preparation, sale, distribution and logistics meaning that they are a one-stop shop for everything from the first sketches to the final sale. Their philosophy is based upon "the respect for the individuality of each pupil. Our collections should give children a feeling of security and association within a community."

Clockwise from left — **Abigail Brown** 2008, *Fox Mask, Rabbit Mask, Bear Mask* Design / Abigail Brown Photography / Graeme McAulay Material / Paper and ribbon Description / Set of 5 creature mask-making kits.

Top — **Vik Prónsdóttir** 2007, *Baby Seal*
Design / Vík Prjónsdóttir   Photographer / Sonja Þórsdóttir   Manufacturer / Víkurprjón
Material / 100% Icelandic wool.

Bottom — **Kristin Rasmussen** 2008, *Bloom II Felt Crown*   Design / Kristin Rasmussen
Manufacturer / Mette   Material / Felt crown features hand-appliqued 'heart' blossoms and leaves, vintage button, elasticised casing in liberty of London's 'black forty'.

1. — **Coq en Pâte** 2008, *T-shirt Bear cub* Design / Virgo Manufacturer / Coq en Pâte Editions Photography / Coq en Pâte Editions Material / 100% organic cotton.

2 - 5. — **Dante Beatrix** 2008, *Fei-Fei (Panda) Kid's T-Shirt, Percival (Dino) Kid's T-Shirt, Esther (Bunny) Kid's T-Shirt, Dieter (Monkey) Kid's T-Shirt* Manufacturer / Dante Beatrix Material / Cotton.

— 1 —

— 2 —

— 3 —

— 4 —

— 5 —

6 - 8. — **Hikje Janneke Zantinge** 2008, *Bendy neck, Pink belly, Red Crane*
Design / Janneke Zantinge   Manufacturer / Hikje   Material / Felt, cotton
Description / 100% cotton T-shirt, with handcut and machine-sewn felt figures.

9. — 2005, **Pee&Poo** *T-shirt*   Design / Emma Megitt
Manufacturer / Pee&Poo | Kiss&Bajs i Sverige AB   Material / Cotton, screen print.

10. — 2005, *Pee&Poo Boys Brief*   Design / Emma Megitt
Manufacturer / Pee&Poo | Kiss&Bajs i Sverige AB   Material / Cotton, screen print.

11. — 2005, *Pee&Poo Socks*   Design / Emma Megitt
Manufacturer / Pee&Poo | Kiss&Bajs i Sverige AB   Material / Cotton, spandex.

12 - 13. — 2005, *Pee&Poo*   Design / Emma Megitt
Manufacturer / Pee&Poo | Kiss&Bajs i Sverige AB   Material / Cotton plush and polyester fibre filling.

- 6 -

- 7 -

- 8 -

- 9 -

- 10 -

- 11 -

- 12 -

- 13 -

Express Yourself / Dante Beatrix, 100drine, Coq en Pâte

1 - 3. — **Dante Beatrix** 2008, *Yuka (Bee) Little Kid Backpack,*
Rory (Lion) Little Kid Backpack, Dieter Little Kid Backpack
Material / Nylon, metal, leather.

4. — **100drine** 2004, *cartable et trousse*   Design / 100drine
Manufacturer / Sentou Editions   Material / Vinyl.

5. — **Coq en Pâte** 2008, *Backpack Wolf*   Design / Virgo
Manufacturer / Coq en Pâte Editions   Material / 100% organic cotton.

6. — 2008, *School Bag*   Design / Virgo
Manufacturer / Coq en Pâte Editions   Material / 100% organic cotton.

- 1 -

- 2 -

- 4 -

- 3 -

- 5 -

- 6 -

214 / 215

- 1 -

- 4 -

1. — **Coq en Pâte** 2008, *Bib Eat Your Soup* Design / Virgo Photography / Coq en Pâte Editions Manufacturer / Coq en Pâte Editions Material / 100% organic cotton.

2. — 2008, *Bib Crêpe* Design / Tinou Le Joly Sénoville Photography / Coq en Pâte Editions Manufacturer / Coq en Pâte Editions Material / 100% organic cotton.

3. — 2008, *Bib Garden Pea* Design / Virgo Photography / Coq en Pâte Editions Manufacturer / Coq en Pâte Editions Material / 100% organic cotton.

4. — 2008, *Luggage and school bag* Design / Tinou Le Joly Sénoville Photography / Annabelle Adie Manufacturer / Coq en Pâte Editions Material / 100% organic cotton Description / School bag & suitcase Arlequin ; suitcase, vanity case and pouch Fox, designed by Tinou Le Joly Sénoville and inspired by the famous tales of Perrault.

5. — 2008, *Marine bag Gorillas* Design / Virgo Photography / Coq en Pâte Editions Manufacturer / Coq en Pâte Editions Material / 100% organic cotton.

6. — 2008, *Marine bag Giraffe* Design / Virgo Photography / Coq en Pâte Editions Manufacturer / Coq en Pâte Editions Material / 100% organic cotton.

- 2 -

- 3 -

- 5 -

- 6 -

5.5 designers 2008, *La maison en éponge* ^{Design} / <u>5.5 designers</u> ^{Photography} / <u>5.5 designers</u> ^{Manufacturer} / <u>Scotch-Brite™</u> ^{Material} / Sponge and scraper Scotch-Brite™ ^{Description} / To celebrate the 50th anniversary of Scotch-Brite™, 5.5 designers designed the "sponge house", a set of five sponges, each one acts as a pictogram, identifying what the individual sponges should be used for.

Little Twig 2008, *Little Twig line* Design / Lenie Ramos Trent Photography / Natalie Boehm Manufacturer / Little Twig Material / Computer illustration printed on film.

- 1 -

- 2 -

1. — **Lola Goldstein** 2007, *Winter Teapots* ^{Design} / <u>Lola Goldstein, knits by Laura Palacious</u> ^{Manufacturer} / Unlimited handmade teapot and scarf ^{Material} / Ceramic, wool ^{Description} / The utilitarian and heart-warming teapot's cozy is a miniature hand-knit scarf.

2. — 2006, *Nut friend* ^{Design} / <u>Lola Goldstein</u> ^{Photographer} / <u>Guillermo Ueno</u> ^{Manufacturer} / <u>Lola Goldstein</u> ^{Material} / Handmade ceramic doll.

3. — **Shinzi Katoh** 2005, *Paint Club: Petit Cup* ^{Design} / <u>Shinzi Katoh</u> ^{Manufacturer} / <u>© Shinzi Katoh</u> ^{Material} / Ceramic.

4. — 2005, *Paint Club: Salad bowl & plate* ^{Design} / <u>Shinzi Katoh</u> ^{Manufacturer} / <u>© Shinzi Katoh</u> ^{Material} / Ceramic.

5. — **100drine** 2006, *La grande tablée* ^{Design} / <u>100drine</u> ^{Manufacturer} / <u>La corbeille</u> ^{Material} / Porcelain.

6. — 2004, *Les verres de la semaine* ^{Design} / <u>100drine</u> ^{Manufacturer} / <u>Sentou Editions</u> ^{Material} / Glasses.

- 3 -

- 4 -

- 5 -

- 6 -

7. — **Twinkle Kids** 2006, *Twinkle Kids Garden Cake*
Design / <u>Robin Arocha</u> Manufacturer / <u>Twinkle Kids</u>
Material / 100% wool felt exterior.

8. — **100drine** 2005, *Plateau radine* Design / <u>100drine</u>
Manufacturer / <u>Sentou Editions</u> Material / Formica.

9. — 2005, *Plateau tartine* Design / <u>100drine</u>
Manufacturer / <u>Sentou Editions</u> Material / Formica.

10. — **Turnstyle** 2007, *Full Tank Packaging*
Design / <u>Steve Watson</u> Manufacturer / Full Tank Baby Fuel.

– 7 –

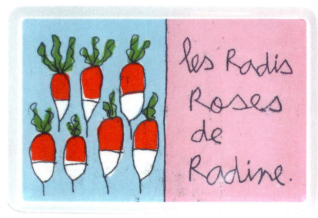

– 8 –

– 9 –

– 10 –

1. — **Irving** 2007, *Two by Two Range*   Design / <u>Julian Roberts & Lucia Gaggiotti</u>   Manufacturer / <u>Artisan Biscuits</u>   Material / Biscuit and cardboard.

2. — 2008, *My Favourite Bear*   Design / <u>Julian Roberts & Brigitte Herrod</u>   Manufacturer / <u>Artisan Biscuits</u>   Material / Printed flow wrap.

3. — **100 drine** 2005, *La boite á bonbons chimioues*   Design / <u>100drine</u>   Manufacturer / <u>Sentou Editions</u>   Material / Metal.

- 1 -

- 2 -

- 3 -

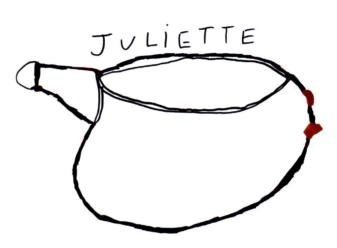

JULIETTE

5.5 designers 2005, *Atelier des enfants au centre Pompidou / Children's workshop Pompidou Centre* Description / Dishes and cutlery treated by children using ceramics, fimo putty and enamel felt marker.

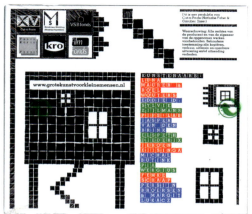

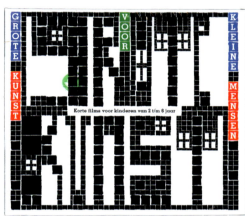

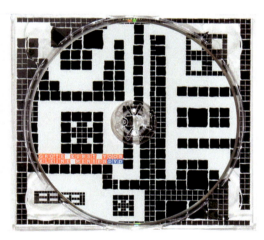

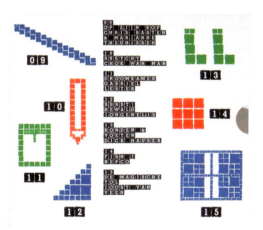

Opposite page — **Jean Jullien** 2008, *La Fontaine* ^{Design /}
Jean Jullien ^{Material} / Paper ^{Description} / Poster about the fables of Jean de la Fontaine, for the La Fontaine exhibition organised at St. Martin's Cyber Café.

Niessen & de Vries 2005, *Grote Kunst voor Kleine Mensen* ^{Manufacturer} / Cut 'n Paste ^{Material} / Offset print, DVD.

1. — **Anorak Magazine** 2007, *Colour in Fashion (spread for Colour in Winter issue)* ^{Design} / Simon Peplow

2. — 2006, *Anorak Launch issue cover* ^{Design} / Supermundane ^{Description} / Cover for the launch issue.

3. — 2007, *Cover December 07 issue* ^{Design} / Supermundane ^{Description} / The COLOUR-IN issue.

4. — 2007, *Cover Spring 07* ^{Design} / Supermundane ^{Description} / The WATER issue.

5. — 2008, *Cover Spring 08* ^{Design} / Supermundane ^{Description} / The MUSIC issue.

6. — 2007, *Cover Anorak Autumn 07* ^{Design} / Supermundane ^{Description} / The SCARED issue.

7. — 2008, *Anorak Cover Summer 08* ^{Design} / Supermundane ^{Description} / The TRAVEL issue.

- 1 -

- 2 -

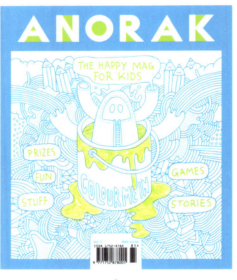

- 3 -

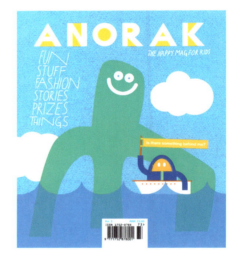

- 4 -

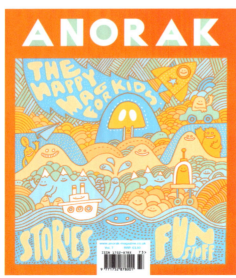

- 5 -

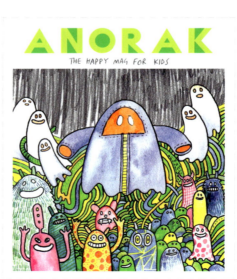

- 6 -

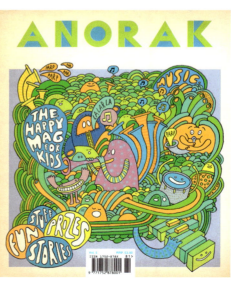

- 7 -

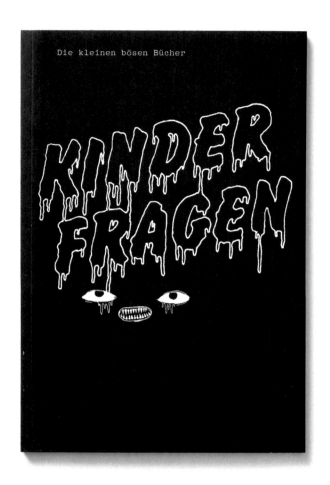

Tobias Röttger 2008, *Die kleinen bösen Bücher / Kinderfragen (The small evil books / children questions)* ^{Design} / Tobias Röttger, Anna Haas.

JUNO GmbH & Co. KG 2005-2008, *Hamburger Museumskindertag* ^{Design} / <u>Eva Kreuzer, Kerstin Bierstedt, Miriam Nehr, Nicole Klein, Sebastian Schneider, Tri Vu, Viktoria Klein, Wolfgang Greter</u> ^{Material} / Paper ^{Description} / Programme and poster for the 'Hamburger Museumskindertag'.

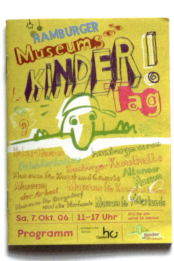

Patric Sandri 2006, *L`hippocampe cherche* ^{Design} / <u>Patric Sandri</u>
^{Photography} / <u>Theres Bütler, James Perret</u> ^{Material} / Acrylic, paper, photography
^{Description} / Book for children between 4 and 10 years. Story about love, loneliness, friendship, self-efficacy. 24 pages, 55 x 31.5 cm (double-page spread).

Mais notre hippocampe ne nage
pas assez
rapidement pour pouvoir les suivre. Ça le rend triste
parce qu'il n'a pas
de camarade pour jouer, rire et parler.

Ah voilà!
Au fond de la mer notre hippocam
surprend une coquille
vachement belle!

dans l'ombre dans la jungle marine,
l'hippocampe soupçonne que la lumière brillante
provient d'une coquille
ouverte
« Comment tu t'appelles? »
« Viens vite! c'est trop dangereux
pour toi, la nuit »
répond-elle seulement

Au dernier moment l'hippocampe
s'est mis à l'abri dans
coquille

Pendant la nuit l'amour et l'hippocampe
bavardent jusqu'à ce qu'ils s'endorment.

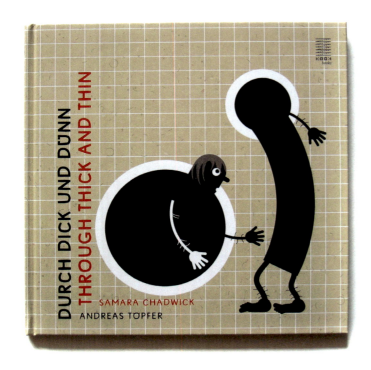

Andreas Töpfer 2007, *Durch Dick und Dünn / Through Thick and Thin* Design / Andreas Töpfer Photography / Katja Zimmermann, Andreas Töpfer Manufacturer / kookbocks Material / Book and a version of the book for iPhone and iPod touch Description / «Through thick and thin» is a picture book to read to children ages 4 and up, and to read alonefrom 6 on. Since Pipa speaks German and Pim speaks English they take turns telling their story, each of them in their own way.

- 1 -

- 2 -

1. — **Judith Drews** 2008, *Frankfurt* ^{Design} / <u>Judith Drews</u> ^{Material} / Print ^{Description} / Schoolbook.

2. — 2008, *Ahoi* ^{Design} / <u>Judith Drews</u> ^{Material} / Silkscreen print on paper ^{Description} / Poster for kids (limited Edition).

3. — 2007, *Zoo* ^{Design} / <u>Judith Drews</u> ^{Material} / Silkscreen print ^{Description} / Poster for children (limited edition).

- 3 -

...LOVE IS ALL...

CATALINA·ESTRADA·

fin!

Catalina Estrada Uribe 2007, *Love is all*   Design / Catalina Estrada
Manufacturer / Unicef   Description / Postcard.

INDEX

A – B

🖊 : Designer / Artist   📷 : Photographer   🏭 : Manufacturer / Brand   ↳ : Web

✏ : Designer / Artist   📷 : Photographer   🏭 : Manufacturer / Brand   ↳ : Web

Boodalee 2007, *p. 163*
✏ : Boodalee
📷 : Mark Adams
🏭 : Boodalee, Boodalee by blik
↳ : www.boodalee.com

Brio 1953 – 2008, *pp. 24, 31*
✏ : Brio
🏭 : Brio AB
↳ : www.brio.net

BTU Cottbus, Lehrstuhl Plastisches Gestalten
     2008, *pp. 68 – 69*
✏ : Linda Bley, Stefan Schreck,
     Tania Coelho, Prof. Jo Achermann,
     Gert Bendel, Karsten Meyer
📷 : Lehrstuhl Plastisches Gestalten,
     BTU Cottbus
↳ : www.tu-cottbus.de/btu/fak2/plagest

Bureau Mario Lombardo 2008, 2007
     pp. 151, 205
✏ : Bureau Mario Lombardo,
     Tania Parovic, Mario Lombardo [(p. 205)]
📷 : Markus Mrugalla
🏭 : Bureau Mario Lombardo
↳ : www.mariolombardo.com

cardboardesign 2004, 2008, *pp. 50, 130*
✏ : Paul Martin [(p. 50)], Ben Blanc [(p. 130)]
📷 : Paul Martin [(p. 50)],
     Cathy Henzy [(p. 130)]
↳ : www.cardboardesign.com

Carton Chic 2007, *p. 53*
✏ : Clara Courtaigne
📷 : Gaetan Bernard
🏭 : Carton Chic
↳ : www.cartonchic.fr

Carve 2005 – 2007, *pp. 70 – 73*
✏ : Carve
📷 : Elger Blitz, Millan van der Storm
🏭 : Carve, Metaplus,
     Playpoint Singapore
↳ : www.carve.nl

Catalina Estrada Uribe 2007, *p. 232*
✏ : Catalina Estrada Uribe
🏭 : Unicef
↳ : www.catalinaestrada.com

cercadelcielo Estudio 2007, *pp. 101*
✏ : cercadelcielo / Joaquin Contreras
📷 : David Frutos
↳ : www.cercadelcielo.es

Chris Woebken 2008, *pp. 184 – 185*
✏ : Chris Woebken, Kenichi Okada
↳ : www.chriswoebken.com

Company 2007, 2008, 2006 – 2007
     pp. 136, 204, 206 – 207
✏ : Company (Aamu Song & Johan Olin)
📷 : Lee Inhee
🏭 : Company
↳ : www.com-pa-ny.com

Coq en Pâte 2008, *pp. 212, 214 – 215*
✏ : Virgo, Tinou Le Joly Sénoville [(p. 217)]
📷 : Coq en Pâte, Annabelle Adie [(p. 217)]
🏭 : Coq en Pâte Editions
↳ : www.coqenpate.com

Corraini Edizioni 1967 / 2008, *p. 131*
✏ : Enzo Mari
🏭 : Corraini Edizioni
↳ : www.corraini.com

Cubeecraft 2008, *p. 52*
✏ : Christopher Beaumont & others
📷 : Chris and Marisa
↳ : www.cubeecraft.com

Dante Beatrix 2008, *p. 212, 214*
✏ : Hester Worst, Jantien Baas
🏭 : Dante Beatrix
↳ : www.dantebeatrix.com

De La Espada 2008 – 2009, *pp. 121, 126*
✏ : Leif.designpark
🏭 : Atlantico
↳ : www.delaespada.com

Delphine Chanet 2004 – 2008, *pp. 196 – 197*
📷 : Delphine Chanet
↳ : www.delphinechanet.com

die Baupiloten 2003 – 2007, *pp. 106 – 111*
✏ : die Baupiloten
📷 : Jan Bitter
↳ : www.baupiloten.com

Dorte Mandrup Arkitekter 2005, *pp. 66 – 67*
✏ : Dorte Mandrup Arkitekter
📷 : Jens Markus Lindhe
↳ : www.dortemandrup.dk

E-Glue 2007 – 2008, *pp. 158 – 161*
✏ : Marielle Baldelli,
     Sébastien Messerschmidt
🏭 : e-glue | adhesive design for kids
↳ : www.e-glue.fr

Elisabeth Dunker → LULA

Emily Gobeille & Theodore Watson 2007,
     pp. 88 – 89
✏ : Emily Gobeille, Theodore Watson
↳ : www.zanyparad.com

Esthex 2007 – 2008, *p. 33*
✏ : Esther Schuivens
📷 : Rob Truijen
🏭 : Esthex
↳ : www.esthex.com

✏ : Designer / Artist   📷 : Photographer   🏭 : Manufacturer / Brand   ↳ : Web

✏ : Designer / Artist   ◎ : Photographer   🏭 : Manufacturer / Brand   ↳ : Web

Judith Zaugg 2005, *pp. 147, 148*
✏ : Judith Zaugg
◎ : Rolf Siegenthaler
🏭 : with Tiger Romig [(p. 148)]
↳ : www.judithzaugg.ch

JUNO 2008, *pp. 226 – 227*
✏ : Eva Kreuzer, Kerstin Bierstedt,
    Miriam Nehr, Nicole Klein,
    Sebastian Schneider, Tri Vu,
    Viktoria Klein, Wolfgang Greter
↳ : www.juno-hamburg.com

Kashiwa Sato 2004 – 2008, *pp. 90 – 93*
✏ : Kashiwa Sato
◎ : Mikiya Sato
↳ : http://kashiwasato.com

Katrin Olina Petursdottir 2005, *p. 130*
✏ : Katrin Olina
◎ : swedese
🏭 : swedese
↳ : www.katrin-olina.com

Kideko 2007, *p. 141*
✏ : Kirsty Bruce
◎ : Tim Robinson
🏭 : Kideko
↳ : www.kideko.com

Kidsonroof 2006, *p. 50*
✏ : Ilya Yashkin
↳ : www.kidsonroof.com

Kleine Burgen 2007 – 2009, *p. 52*
✏ : Olaf Hoffmann
↳ : www.kleineburgen.de

Kloss 2007, *pp. 127, 135*
✏ : Ole Petter Wullum
🏭 : Kloss
↳ : www.kloss.no

KOON Co. 2004 – 2008, *pp. 122, 128 – 129, 130, 134*
✏ : Aracho,
    Hye Young Park
    Young Woo Kim & Seung Heum Park
    Ji Yoon Jeong & Young Hee Lee
🏭 : KOON, Little KooN
↳ : www.koondesign.com

Kristian Kutschera 2008, *pp. 54, 118*
✏ : Kristian Kutschera
◎ : bürokutschera
↳ : www.kristiankutschera.de

Kristin Rasmussen 2008, *p. 211*
✏ : Kristin Rasmussen
🏭 : Mette
↳ : www.mette.ca

LAN Architecture 2008, *p. 100*
✏ : LAN Architecture
◎ : Jean-Marie Monthiers
↳ : www.lan-paris.com

Lizette Greco 2006, *pp. 11,*
✏ : Lizette Greco and Grecolaborativo
◎ : Paper
↳ : www.grecolaborativo.com

Life Time Furniture 2007, *pp. 132-133*
✏ : Hester Worst, Jantien Baas
◎ : Ede Lukkien
🏭 : M. Schack Engels A/S
↳ : www.lifetime-furniture.com

Little Twig 2008, *p. 217*
✏ : Lenie Ramos Trent
◎ : Natalie Boehm
🏭 : Little Twig
↳ : www.littletwig.com

Lola Goldstein 2006, 2007, *p. 218*
✏ : Lola Goldstein,
    knits Laura Palacious
◎ : Guillermo Ueno
↳ : www.muitotosto.com/lola

Lorena Siminovich 2006 – 2008, *pp. 148 – 149*
✏ : Lorena Siminovich
◎ : Annie Tsou
🏭 : Petit Collage
↳ : www.petitcollage.com

LULA 2007 – 2008, *pp. 56 – 59, 114 – 115, 202 – 203*
✏ : Elisabeth Dunker,
    Little Red Stuga Design studio
    Ulrika Engberg [(pp. 114–115)]
◎ : Elisabeth Dunker
🏭 : Little Red Stuga [(pp. 114–115)]
    Petit and Small Magazine [(pp. 202–203)]
↳ : www.lula.se

Marcus Walters 2008, *pp. 26, 232 – 233*
✏ : Marcus Walters
↳ : www.marcuswalters.com

Marije Vogelzang | Proef 2007, *pp. 190 – 193*
✏ : Marije Vogelzang
↳ : www.proefamsterdam.nl

Marilyn Neuhart 2007, *pp. 8 – 9*
✏ : Marilyn Neuhart
◎ : Andrew Neuhart

Marine Duroselle 2007, *p. 175*
◎ : Marine Duroselle
↳ : marineduroselle.com

Martino Gamper 2003, *p. 128*
✏ : Martino Gamper
↳ : www.gampermartino.com

✎ : Designer / Artist   ◻ : Photographer   ⚒ : Manufacturer / Brand   ↳ : Web

S – Z

PLAY ALL DAY

Design for Children

Edited by **Robert Klanten, Sven Ehmann**
Cover and layout by **Floyd Schulze** for Gestalten
Preface and chapter introductions by **Ole Wagner** for Gestalten
Project descriptions by **Shonquis Moreno** for Gestalten
Cover photography by **Jan von Holleben**

Project management: **Julian Sorge** for Gestalten
Production management: **Janine Milstrey**, **Martin Bretschneider** for Gestalten
Proofreading: **Patricia Mehnert**
Printed by **Offsetdruckerei Grammlich, Pliezhausen**
Made in Germany

Published by **Gestalten**, Berlin 2009
ISBN 978-3-89955-236-2

For more information, please check www.gestalten.com

Bibliographic information published by the Deutsche Nationalbibliothek.
The Deutsche Nationalbibliothek lists this publication in the Deutsche Nationalbibliografie;
detailed bibliographic data is available on the internet at http://dnb.d-nb.de.

None of the content in this book was published in exchange for payment by commercial parties
or designers; Gestalten selected all included work based solely on its artistic merit.

This book was printed according to the internationally accepted FSC standards for environmental protection, which specify requirements for an environmental management system.

Mixed Sources
Product group from well-managed
forests and other controlled sources
www.fsc.org Cert no. IMO-COC-028001
© 1996 Forest Stewardship Council

Gestalten is a climate neutral company and so are our products. We collaborate with the non-
profit carbon offset provider myclimate (www.myclimate.org) to neutralize the company's carbon footprint produced through our worldwide business activities by investing in projects that
reduce CO_2 emissions (www.gestalten.com/myclimate).